Proxmox High Availability

Introduce, design, and implement high availability clusters using Proxmox

Simon M.C. Cheng

BIRMINGHAM - MUMBAI

Proxmox High Availability

First published: October 2014

Production reference: 1241014

Published by Packt Publishing Ltd.
Livery Place
35 Livery Street
Birmingham B3 2PB, UK.

ISBN 978-1-78398-088-8

www.packtpub.com

Cover image by Suyog Gharat (yogiee@me.com)

Credits

Author
Simon M.C. Cheng

Reviewers
Alessio Bravi
David Fischer
Philip Iezzi
Damien PIQUET

Commissioning Editor
Kartikey Pandey

Acquisition Editor
Subho Gupta

Content Development Editor
Ruchita Bhansali

Technical Editor
Aman Preet Singh

Copy Editors
Karuna Narayanan
Alfida Paiva

Project Coordinator
Kranti Berde

Proofreaders
Simran Bhogal
Maria Gould
Paul Hindle

Indexer
Rekha Nair

Graphics
Sheetal Aute
Ronak Dhruv
Valentina D'silva
Disha Haria
Abhinash Sahu

Production Coordinator
Nilesh R. Mohite

Cover Work
Adonia Jones
Nilesh R. Mohite

About the Author

Simon M.C. Cheng is an experienced engineer and has been working in the field of system administration on Linux and Windows platforms for around 8 years. He has a Bachelor's degree in Computing from The Hong Kong Polytechnic University.

He currently lives in Hong Kong and has previously worked in a number of different roles, including as a technician at a college, IT officer at Geodis Wilson Hong Kong Limited, senior systems engineer at Questex Media Limited and Ignite Media Group, and a few more roles. In recent years, he has become interested in server virtualization and has put his efforts into learning more about it.

If you have anything to share, you can contact him on LinkedIn or e-mail him at `simonc1001@hotmail.com`.

I am deeply indebted to my acquisition editors, Ashish Bhanushali and Subho Gupta, and the project co-ordinator, Kinjal Bari, who gave me the chance to write my first book. It was a great gamble for them to choose me because I had no prior experience in book publishing.

I would like to express my deepest gratitude to my responsible editor, Ruchita Bhansali. She is a very helpful and responsible editor who put in a lot of effort in this book and led me through the process of publishing this book.

I am also grateful to all the reviewers from different technical backgrounds for their comments, opinions, and valuable suggestions for this book. These suggestions have definitely enriched and expanded the content of this book. Thanks to them for making this book interesting and enriching.

Last but not least, I would like to take this opportunity to give credit to my parents and my girlfriend, Fanny. Without their understanding and support, I would not have had the courage to accept this new challenge.

About the Reviewers

Alessio Bravi has been playing with "bits" since he was 5 years old. He started programming at the age of 6, and soon, he started focusing his attention on network administration and IT systems security, in the best period of the Internet age.

When he was 19 years old, he founded IntSec.NET, where he worked as the Chief Technology Officer (CTO). He has also worked as a network and security administrator for Italian Internet Services Providers (ISPs/WISPs) and as an IT security consultant for many companies in Europe.

He works only with Unix-like OSes and specializes in IT security analysis, network engineering and administration, autonomous systems BGP routing, IPv4 and IPv6 routing and switching, OS virtualization, and data center management.

He writes some technical articles to share IT hints with the digital world on his personal blog at http://blog.bravi.org/. More on Alessio's technical skills and personal details can be found on his LinkedIn profile page at http://www.linkedin.com/in/alessiobravi.

David Fischer spent 5 years as a research assistant at Hepia, University of Applied Sciences Geneva, Telecommunications Laboratory, where he focused on building distributed media-oriented platforms, automating the deployment and maintenance of open-source-based network services, and operating cloud-based infrastructures. In the meantime, he got his Master's degree in Information and Communication Technologies. His thesis project, Open Source Cloud Infrastructure for Encoding and Distribution (OSCIED), made in collaboration with the European Broadcasting Union (EBU), was aimed at providing a scalable media open source platform to the members of the EBU. With his colleagues at Sigala Media, based in BC, Canada, Mr. Fischer is now building an advanced cloud transcoding solution called CloudNcode. He lives in Geneva, Switzerland, with his wife, Claire, and child, Eliott.

Philip Iezzi is a Swiss system engineer and web application programmer. He primarily works with Linux server technologies and network security, and has been doing web development since 1999. He devoted a lot of time to open source projects, and he is the author of PowerPhlogger (2000-2006), Pigalle, YaBook, and the Sourdough Application Framework for PHP. In 2003, he founded his own web-hosting company, Onlime Webhosting (https://www.onlime.ch). In 2005, he got his Master's degree in Computer Science and Business Informatics from the University of Zurich, Switzerland.

Currently, he is working at Datenpark as a systems engineer, and spends a lot of time on various web projects, specifically Airpane Controlpanel, a user administration backend and CRM. Airpane Controlpanel, a central software component, is used by the web-hosting companies Onlime Webhosting and Datenpark. After gaining some experience with Java, C#, and .NET at Credit-Suisse, he is now strongly focusing again on PHP development with Zend Framework and Symfony2.

As a systems engineer, he is currently maintaining a large number of Debian Linux servers. For him, Virtualization technology plays an important role, and in a 100 percent Linux environment, Proxmox VE with OpenVZ seems like the perfect solution. He reviewed this book after gaining 2 years of experience in Proxmox VE and more than 4 years in OpenVZ.

Besides being such a technical guy, Philip is also father of his beloved girl Luisa.

Damien PIQUET is a French system administrator with experience in virtualized environments. He started working with Proxmox VE in 2011 and deployed his first cluster infrastructure in 2012. He contributes to Proxmox VE by helping in translating it into French. He is also the creator and maintainer of pve-monitor, a Nagios/Shinken plugin for monitoring Proxmox VE in a cluster; this plugin is available at http://exchange.nagios.org/.

www.PacktPub.com

Support files, eBooks, discount offers, and more

You might want to visit www.PacktPub.com for support files and downloads related to your book.

Did you know that Packt offers eBook versions of every book published, with PDF and ePub files available? You can upgrade to the eBook version at www.PacktPub.com and as a print book customer, you are entitled to a discount on the eBook copy. Get in touch with us at service@packtpub.com for more details.

At www.PacktPub.com, you can also read a collection of free technical articles, sign up for a range of free newsletters and receive exclusive discounts and offers on Packt books and eBooks.

http://PacktLib.PacktPub.com

Do you need instant solutions to your IT questions? PacktLib is Packt's online digital book library. Here, you can access, read and search across Packt's entire library of books.

Why subscribe?

- Fully searchable across every book published by Packt
- Copy and paste, print and bookmark content
- On demand and accessible via web browser

Free access for Packt account holders

If you have an account with Packt at www.PacktPub.com, you can use this to access PacktLib today and view nine entirely free books. Simply use your login credentials for immediate access.

Table of Contents

Preface

Nowadays, the number of network services is rapidly increasing, due to which service availability has become a concern. With the help of the easy-to-use tools provided by Proxmox, users can easily improve their service by building their own clusters. The support of various storage options provides flexibility with different forms of network storage.

What this book covers

Chapter 1, *Basic Concepts of a Proxmox Virtual Environment*, explains the concept of virtualization and compares Proxmox with other virtualization software.

Chapter 2, *Getting Started with a High Availability (HA) Environment*, includes the functions provided by a Proxmox cluster and explains how it achieves high availability.

Chapter 3, *Key Components for Building a Proxmox VE Cluster*, explains all the components required when building a Proxmox cluster environment.

Chapter 4, *Configuring a Proxmox VE Cluster*, demonstrates the actual installation and configuration of a Proxmox cluster.

Chapter 5, *Testing on a Proxmox Cluster*, includes testing on a configured Proxmox cluster.

Chapter 6, *System Migration of an Existing System to a Proxmox VE Cluster*, explains how to migrate existing running systems, including Windows, Linux, and other virtualization software file formats to a Proxmox cluster.

Chapter 7, *Disaster Recovery on a Proxmox VE Cluster*, talks about the backup of a Proxmox cluster. The chapter also introduces the system restore process when a Proxmox cluster fails.

Chapter 8, Troubleshooting on a Proxmox Cluster, introduces all the troubleshooting content.

What you need for this book

The list of hardware components required is given as follows:

- A minimum of two servers are required. Three servers are needed if you want to test a Gluster filesystem.
- A shared storage that is accessible on all the servers as a quorum disk and as VM storage.
- Two network cards on each server.
- Two network switches.

The software needed for this book are as follows:

- Proxmox Virtual Environment 3.2 or above
- NAS4Free 9.2.0.1 or an alternative to build a software-based NAS storage
- DRBD 2:8.3.13-2 or above
- GlusterFS 3.5.1 or above
- CEPH (built with Proxmox)

Who this book is for

This book is intended for those who want to know the secrets of virtualization and how network services provide high availability. This book is suitable for beginners and advanced users who are interested in virtualization and cluster technology. For those who are already using Proxmox, it is a great chance to build a high availability cluster with a distributed filesystem to further protect your server system from failure. If you are a beginner, this book also gets you up to speed on what is happening from conception to implementation. For this book, it will be better if you have some experience in network and system administration, while experience in Proxmox is not necessary.

Conventions

In this book, you will find a number of styles of text that distinguish between different kinds of information. Here are some examples of these styles, and an explanation of their meaning.

Code words in text, database table names, folder names, filenames, file extensions, pathnames, dummy URLs, user input, and Twitter handles are shown as follows: "Create a new file under /etc/init.d/tty.conf with vi or any text editor you like."

A block of code is set as follows:

```
<fencedevices>
  <fencedevice agent="fence_ifmib" community="Mycluster_community"
    ipaddr="192.168.1.45" name="fence_ifmib_SW1" snmp_version="2c" />
  <fencedevice agent="fence_ifmib" community="Mycluster_community"
    ipaddr="192.168.1.46" name="fence_ifmib_SW2" snmp_version="2c" />
</fencedevices>
```

When we wish to draw your attention to a particular part of a code block, the relevant lines or items are set in bold:

```
</rm>
  <failoverdomains>
    <failoverdomain name="myfailover" nofailback="1" ordered="1"
      restricted="1">
        <failoverdomainnode name="vmsrv01" priority="1"/>
        <failoverdomainnode name="vmsrv02" priority="2"/>
    </failoverdomain>
  </failoverdomains>
  <pvevm>
```

Any command-line input or output is written as follows:

```
sudo apt-get install lshw
```

New terms and **important words** are shown in bold. Words that you see on the screen, in menus or dialog boxes for example, appear in the text like this: "Click on the **Content** tab and choose **Templates**, as shown in the following screenshot:"

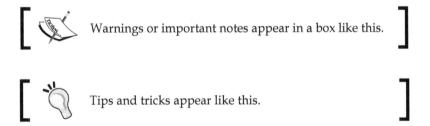

Warnings or important notes appear in a box like this.

Tips and tricks appear like this.

Reader feedback

Feedback from our readers is always welcome. Let us know what you think about this book—what you liked or may have disliked. Reader feedback is important for us to develop titles that you really get the most out of.

To send us general feedback, simply send an e-mail to `feedback@packtpub.com`, and mention the book title via the subject of your message.

If there is a topic that you have expertise in and you are interested in either writing or contributing to a book, see our author guide on `www.packtpub.com/authors`.

Customer support

Now that you are the proud owner of a Packt book, we have a number of things to help you to get the most from your purchase.

Errata

Although we have taken every care to ensure the accuracy of our content, mistakes do happen. If you find a mistake in one of our books—maybe a mistake in the text or the code—we would be grateful if you would report this to us. By doing so, you can save other readers from frustration and help us improve subsequent versions of this book. If you find any errata, please report them by visiting `http://www.packtpub.com/submit-errata`, selecting your book, clicking on the **errata submission form** link, and entering the details of your errata. Once your errata are verified, your submission will be accepted and the errata will be uploaded on our website, or added to any list of existing errata, under the Errata section of that title. Any existing errata can be viewed by selecting your title from `http://www.packtpub.com/support`.

Piracy

Piracy of copyright material on the Internet is an ongoing problem across all media. At Packt, we take the protection of our copyright and licenses very seriously. If you come across any illegal copies of our works, in any form, on the Internet, please provide us with the location address or website name immediately so that we can pursue a remedy.

Please contact us at `copyright@packtpub.com` with a link to the suspected pirated material.

We appreciate your help in protecting our authors, and our ability to bring you valuable content.

Questions

You can contact us at `questions@packtpub.com` if you are having a problem with any aspect of the book, and we will do our best to address it.

1

Basic Concepts of a Proxmox Virtual Environment

Have you ever imagined how good it would be if you don't need to stop your services during a system upgrade operation? Do you have a powerful server but haven't used all of its resources? Do you want to set up a server platform quickly using a system template? If the answer to all these questions is yes, then you will be very happy to work with **Proxmox Virtual Environment** (also called **Proxmox VE**).

This chapter will show you some basic concepts of Proxmox VE before actually using it, including the technology used, basic administration, and some options available during set up.

The following topics are going to be covered in this chapter:

- An explanation of server virtualization used by Proxmox VE
- An introduction of basic administrative tools available in Proxmox VE
- An explanation of different virtualization modes and storage options

Introduction to Proxmox Virtual Environment

So what is Proxmox Virtual Environment actually used for? Proxmox VE is an open source bare metal environment based on the Debian Linux distribution (also called **hypervisor** or **Virtual Machine Monitor** (**VMM**)) for server virtualization. It allows a user to install different operating systems (for example, Windows, Linux, Unix, and others) on a single computer or a cluster built by grouping computers together. It consists of powerful Kernel-based virtual machines and lightweight OpenVZ containers as an alternative.

The main features for Proxmox VE can be summarized as follows:

- **Open source**: It is fully open source under General Public License, version 3 (GNU AGPL, v3), which means you can freely view, alter, and remove the source code, and distribute your own version as long as you are compliant with the license.

- **Live migration**: This allows moving a running virtual machine from one physical server to another without downtime.

- **High availability**: In Proxmox HA cluster mode, when one node fails, the remaining virtual machines will be moved to a healthy node to make sure there is minimal service interruption.

- **Bridged networking**: Proxmox VE allows a user to build a private network between the virtual machines. VLAN options are also available.

- **Flexible storage**: A wide range of storage options are available, including both local and network-based storage technologies such as LVM, iSCSI, NFS, the Gluster filesystem, and the CEPH filesystem.

- **OS template**: Proxmox VE allows users to build their own OS template for further deployment. Of course, it is also possible for users to download a template file from the Internet and import that file into their system.

- **Scheduled backup**: A user interface is provided to users so that they can set up their own backup strategy. The backup files can be stored locally or on any supported storage option that you have configured.

- **Command-line (CLI) tool**: Proxmox VE provides different CLI management tools allowing users to access the virtual machine container, manage resources, and so on.

 You can try Proxmox for free at `http://pve.proxmox.com/wiki/Downloads`.

Introduction to server virtualization

Have you ever heard about *cloud computing*? It is a hot topic in the IT industry and claims that you can allocate nearly unlimited computer resources on a pay-as-you-go basis. Are you not curious to know how they are able to provide such a service? The underlying technology that allows them to be able to provide such a service is hardware virtualization. If you don't understand how virtualization works, it could be difficult for you to imagine how they can add or remove resources instantly. Let's talk about how server virtualization works and what it offers us.

Why should we use server virtualization? Since the new generation of server class machines are becoming much more powerful, it becomes quite difficult to use up all the system resources if we only install one **Operating System (OS)** on it. Also, renting multiple server racks in a data center is expensive. Centralizing multiple servers into a limited set of powerful servers seems to be a more cost-effective solution, thus virtualization appears. Server virtualization allows users to create multiple system objects called **virtual machines** (**VMs**) that act like normal computers. Virtualization of physical devices implies that each virtual machine has its own CPU units (called vCPU), memory, hard disk, and network card, according to a user's allocation. When the user turns on the virtual machines, different OSes can be installed on them. Therefore, *better system resources utilization* can be achieved. The following figure shows the difference between a physical machine and a virtual machine:

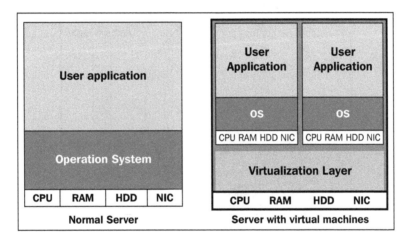

Depending on the kind of processor used, there are three different types of virtualizations available: **full virtualization**, **para-virtualization**, and **hardware-assisted virtualization**. In order to state the difference between these virtualization methods, we need to know how a Control Processing Unit (CPU) executes code that a user has passed.

During any process execution, a CPU is the computing unit that executes predefined instruction sets to generate the results that the program had defined. But, it is dangerous if we give full access to all applications on our devices. For example, if there is no restriction on hardware access, a web page will be able to inject suspicious code into local memory and it may further damage the data stored in our computers. Therefore, a term called *protection ring ranking*, which ranges from 0 to 3 under the x86 architecture is used to protect our hardware. Normally, **Ring 0** (also called **supervisor mode**) is used in the OS to monitor and control system resources. **Ring 3** (also called **user mode**) is used for a user application, and if we would like to have access to hardware, a system call provided from the supervisor mode must be made. The following figure shows the system ring structure for the x86 platform:

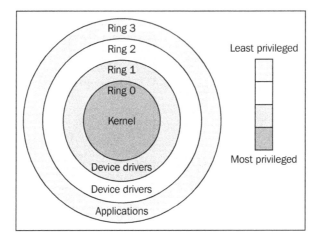

Based on the levels of virtualization, we have the following different types of virtualization types: full virtualization, para-virtualization, and hardware-assisted virtualization:

- **Full virtualization**: In this the VMM is placed under *Ring 0* while the virtualized guest OS is installed under *Ring 1*. However, some system calls can only be executed under Ring 0. Therefore, a process called **binary translation** is used to translate such system calls, and thus, the performance is degraded. In this mode, the guest OS does not know it is being virtualized, so it does not require kernel modification. Here is a simple structure for this type of virtualization:

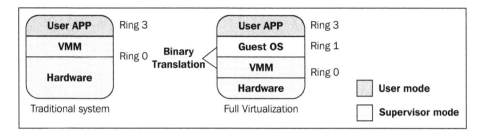

- **Para-virtualization**: This is very similar to full virtualization, but *custom drivers* are installed on the guest OS in order to access CPU resources without downgrading to **Ring 1**. So, the performance of the guest OS is near to that of the physical machine because the translation process is not needed, but the guest OS requires a modified kernel. Thus, the guest cannot run a different operating system from the host operation system. The following diagram shows the structure of this virtualization:

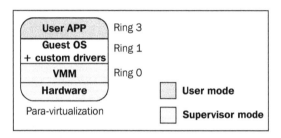

- **Hardware-assisted virtualization**: CPU manufacturers introduce a new functionality for a virtualized platform, Intel VT-x and AMD-V. The ring level 0 to 3 is categorized into **non-root** modes, and a new level, -1, is introduced as the **root mode**. The guest OS is now installed to **Ring 0**, which means it can access hardware directly. Because it does not need a custom API to make system calls under **Ring 0**, no kernel modification is needed. The following diagram shows you the structure of the virtualization mode:

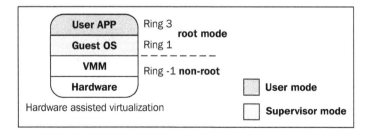

Server virtualization basics – guest versus host

So, when both physical and virtualized platforms are running operating systems, how can we distinguish them from each other? Here come the terms: host and guest, explained in the following points:

- **Host OS**: It is an operating system that provides virtualization capabilities for creation, modification, and removal of virtual machines. A virtualization package contains a component called **Virtual Machine Monitor**, which provides an isolated environment to run multiple platforms.

- **Guest OS**: This refers to the operating system installed inside the virtual environment. The supported guest OS depends on the virtualization software, and the performance of the guest OS depends on how many resources have been allocated to it. The following diagram shows a simple diagram on how we assign different system resources to our virtual machines:

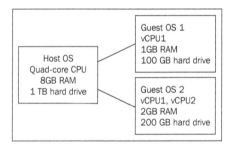

Comparing types of server virtualization software

We have discussed why we need to learn server virtualization and how virtualization works, so are you curious about how many types of major virtualization software are on the market? What are the differences between them? Let's take a deep look at it:

- **Proxmox VE**: As mentioned before, Proxmox VE is an open source hypervisor based on GNU/Linux (Debian-based) with a RHEL-based kernel and published under **GNU AGPL v3**. It differs from the alternative virtualization software as Proxmox provides a central web-based management without further installation. The underlying technologies used are **Open Virtuozzo (OpenVZ)** and **Kernel-based Virtual Machine (KVM)**, which will be described in Version 1.6. Subscription plans are available for accessing enterprise repository, software updates, and user support.

- **XenServer**: This is a native hypervisor based on GNU/Linux developed by the Xen Project and published under **GNU AGPL v2** as open source. For XenServer, a concept of **domain** is used for all virtual machines, and the most privileged domain (for example, a domain that allows direct access to hardware) — **dom0**, is used by the hypervisor to manage other **domU** virtual machines. It supports para-virtualization, which allows a user to run virtualized guests on a CPU without support for virtualization; for example, no Intel VT-x or AMD-V is needed. Amazon Web Service (AWS) is a production example of using XenServer.

- **VMware ESX/ESXi**: This is a bare-metal hypervisor developed by VMware based on a customized kernel called **vmkernel**, which is a microkernel developed by VMware.

  The difference between ESX and ESXi is that ESXi is a free version of ESX with some resource limitations. ESX has a hardware compatibility list that includes many drivers for network cards and SCSI cards. An extra hardware driver can be added to the base installation if needed. On top of the para-virtualization and hardware-assisted virtualization, ESX provides full virtualization as another option.

  There are two management tools available: **vSphere client** and **vCenter server**. VSphere client is enough for normal administration operation on one ESX while vCenter server allows the user to manage multiple ESXs, including the configuration of advanced features such as **high availability** and **live migration**.

- **Hyper-V server**: This is a proprietary virtualization platform produced by Microsoft Corporation running under the Windows platform starting from Windows Server 2008. If you are mainly using a Windows platform as your virtualized guest, it is recommended that you use Hyper-V, especially if you have enabled an Active Directory domain services.

  Hyper-V provides better migration options to users; it not only provides live migration, but also provides *unlimited guest movements between hosts*. The benefit of the features of an Active Directory domain is that Hyper-V provides *replica on virtual machines*, which allows a user to copy a specific VM from the source's site to the target site asynchronously via a WAN or a secure VPN.

Comparison table of hypervisors

We have learned that there are many virtualization platforms on the market, so what are the differences between them? Let's take a look at the following table:

Virtualization platform	Proxmox	XenServer	VMware ESX/ESXi	Hyper-V server
Latest version	3.2	6.1	5.5	Server 2012 R2
License	GNU GPL v3	GNU GPL v2	Proprietary	Free
Open Source	Yes	Yes	No	No
Base OS	Linux	Linux	Vmkernel	Windows
Console OS	No	Yes	Yes	No
Management tools	Web GUI	XenCenter	vSphere Client vCenter	Hyper-V Manager
Host HA	Yes	Yes	Yes (vCenter)	Yes
Guest HA	Yes	Yes, (XenMotion)	Yes, (vMotion)	Yes (Live Migration)
Supported storage	LVM groupNFS, iSCSI, RBD, NAS, and SAS	NFS, iSCSI, fiber channel, NAS, SAS, and CIFS	Fibre Channel, iSCSI, NAS, and SAS	SMB, iSCSI, Fibre channel, NAS, and SAS
Supported virtualization technology*	• FV (KVM) • OpenVZ	• PV • HV	• FV • PV • HV	• PV • HV
License model	Per CPU	Per CPU	Per CPU	Per VM and host

In the previous table, FV stands for full virtualization, PV stands for para-virtualization, and HV stands for hardware-assisted virtualization.

Basic administration on Proxmox VE

After we have talked about so many concepts, let's learn how to configure Proxmox! I assume you have downloaded and installed your own Proxmox. If you face any difficulty during the installation, you can refer to the following link:

```
https://pve.proxmox.com/wiki/Quick_installation
```

The following steps will help you perform basic administration in Proxmox VE:

1. After the installation, you should be able to see the following screen:

2. In this step, access the Proxmox VE using a web browser, and make sure you have network access and you are connected in the same subnet as Proxmox. Then, type in a URL in the following format in your browser: `https://<Proxmox_IP>:8006`. When you first visit the page, your browser will warn you that the SSL certificate is not a trusted one. It is normal if you have experience in building your self-signed SSL certificate on your web server. If you have a domain name for your Proxmox server and would like to have a SSL certificate signed by an authorized CA, please take a look at the following sites:

    ◦ Apache CSR creation using OpenSSL `http://www.digicert.com/csr-creation-apache.htm`

    ◦ HTTPS certificate configuration `http://pve.proxmox.com/wiki/HTTPSCertificateConfiguration`

3. Next, simply choosing **Continue to this website** in Internet Explorer adds to the exception. Similarly, choose **I understand the risk** in Firefox and Chrome. Next, just log in to the system with the root account since we haven't created our own user account. Being logged in, the following warning message indicates that you do not have a valid subscription plan. You can ignore this warning message if you currently don't need to have technical support.

4. Within the web GUI, you will be able to manage most features of the Proxmox platform. For example, you can create new virtual machines by using the buttons located in the upper-right corner, as shown in the following screenshot:

There are two ways to create new virtual machines: **Create VM** and **Create CT**.

5. By clicking on the **Create CT** button, you can create a *virtualized Linux platform* under the OpenVZ *container*. It is recommended for GNU/Linux guests because the Linux kernel is shared with the host server, which means that the used memory on the host server will be reduced. When you go through the wizard after clicking on the **Create CT** button, a virtualized OS is created based on the **OS template** you used. An OS template is an operation system (for example, CentOS, Debian, and others) with customized packages installed and predefined system parameters. The templates are available in the form of a brand new system or installed with a web server or an application like Drupal. Typically, no **graphical user interface (GUI)** is preinstalled in the virtualized guests if you use this type of installation.

Uploading the OS template or the ISO file to Proxmox

Before we can start trying to build our own virtual machines with OpenVZ, we have to first upload either an OS template or an ISO file that contains the operating system installation files to Proxmox. The following steps will help us understand how to do this:

1. Double-click on the icon that is named as the hostname of Proxmox, then choose **local**, click on **Content**, and choose **Upload** from the panel on the right-hand side, as shown in the following screenshot:

2. After we have clicked on the **Upload** button, three options are available, as shown in the following screenshot:

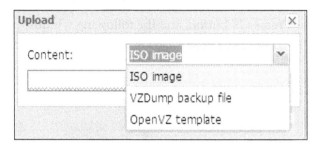

The three options available are as follows:

- **ISO image**: This is used as the installation source file for Kernel-based virtualization
- **VZDump backup file**: This is used to upload backup files created by Proxmox for restoration
- **OpenVZ template**: This is used for the installation source for OpenVZ virtualization

3. Then, we can simply browse the file that we would like to upload. Pay attention when uploading the OpenVZ template file; you need to use the following naming format:

```
{OSName}-{OSVersion}-{OSName}_{OSType}_{amd64/i386}.tar.gz
```

This format is shown in the following example:

```
centos-6-CentOS_standard_amd64.tar.gz
```

The output can be seen in the following screenshot:

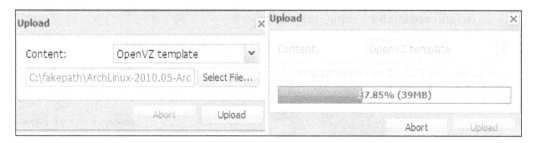

We are now ready to create our own virtual machines; let's see how we can create an OpenVZ-based virtual machine first. For example, the OpenVZ template file will be stored inside /var/lib/vz/template/cache/; you can also manually upload it to that directory if you don't wish to use the web interface.

Creating an OpenVZ-based virtual machine

To create an OpenVZ-based virtual machine, please follow these steps:

1. Click on the **Create CT** button, and the following window pops up; a *system hostname* and a password for the root account can be defined, as shown in the following screenshot:

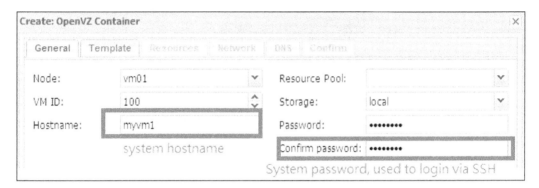

2. Next, the system will ask you for the template you want to use; for example, you can choose **centOS-6-CentOS_devel_amd64.tar.gz**:

3. Then, you will be asked to assign resources to the VM; we can accept the default setting for testing purposes:

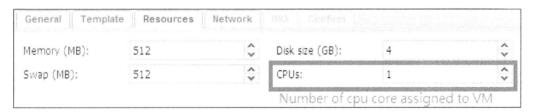

4. After we have allocated system resources to the new virtual machine, we reach an important part: networking. Here, you have the following two options:

   ○ **Routed mode**: This uses the default network interface used by Proxmox, and simply specifies an IP address. Only select routed mode if you create a guest system that lies in the same IP subnet as the host system. It would be slightly easier during the system configuration than in the Bridged mode.

   ○ **Bridged mode**: This allows you to choose a network adapter other than the default one (including a VLAN-enabled interface). It requires a DHCP server for IP assignment or is manually configured under VM. A demonstration on how to configure the Bridged mode will be shown in *Chapter 4, Configuring a Proxmox VE Cluster*.

   In the following screenshot, we choose the **Routed mode** and specify an IP address for demonstration:

5. The following settings regarding the DNS parameters are saved to the /etc/resolv.conf file in the virtualized guest:

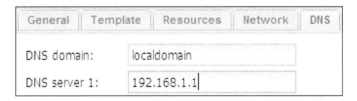

6. A summary for the configuration is displayed before the VM is created.

7. After the VM creation is completed, you can view its status in the **Summary** tab, as shown in the following screenshot:

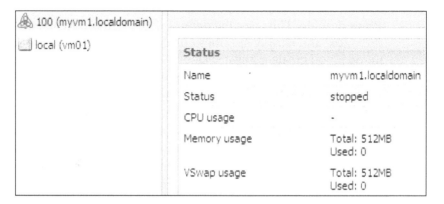

Creating a kernel-based virtual machine

We have seen how to create OpenVZ-based virtual machines; now, let's learn how we can create a kernel-based virtual machine:

1. Click on the **Create VM** button in the top-right corner, as shown in the following screenshot:

2. Specify a name for identification, but please note that the name is not directly applied to the VM's hostname, as shown in the following screenshot:

3. Then, we need to choose the type of platform we are going to create, shown as follows:

4. Next, the OS installation source is specified, shown as follows:

5. After that, we have to allocate the hard disk for the virtual machine. Pay attention to the hard disk's **Format** you have chosen; the raw format will instantly allocate the space you have defined (that is, if you defined a 20 GB hard disk, a disk image with 20 GB will be created under the host server) while the QEMU format will only allocate the space based on the current usage of the guest OS. If the guest OS takes up 8 GB, then a disk image with 8 GB in size will be created. For more details, refer to the *Virtual disk options under Proxmox VE* section. The hard disk window is shown in the following screenshot:

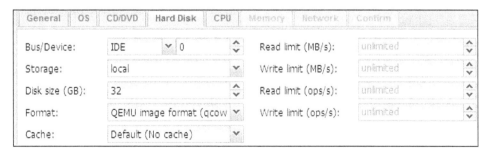

6. The number of cores/sockets and the CPU types have to be specified for the guest, as shown in the following screenshot:

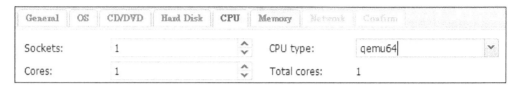

7. Of course, we need to allocate the amount of memory for the guest platform, shown as follows:

8. For the network part, similar to the OpenVZ creation, we have **bridged mode** and **NAT mode**. Here, we can specify **Model** for the virtualized VM; generally, choosing Intel E1000 and Realtek RTL8139 should be fine. The **VirtIO** option provides better performance, but the driver must be installed on the guest OS before it can be used. This is shown in the following screenshot:

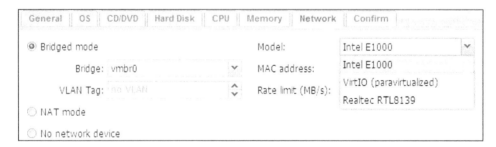

9. A summary of the configurations is displayed for confirmation.

10. Just as it appears for OpenVZ, we can find our created VM under the menu, as follows:

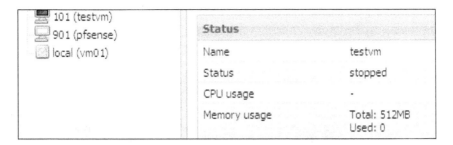

Isn't it easy to create a virtual machine with a web interface? By the way, you can identify whether a virtual machine is an OpenVZ container or KVM by its associated icons, as shown in the following screenshot:

Accessing the new virtual machine

Congratulations! You have just created your own virtual machine! Wait, how can we access the system? That's a good question; here, we have two options to achieve our goal. One option is to access it from the web browser. What? Access an operating system with a web browser? Yes, let's see how it works:

1. Right-click on the virtual machine you would like to access from the panel on the left-hand side, and then choose **console**.

   Prior to Proxmox 3.2, a new console mode, SPICE, was introduced, which provides a better usage performance especially in a KVM machine. You can refer to `https://pve.proxmox.com/wiki/SPICE` for more details.

   Make sure you have the latest JAVA runtime (JRE), preferably with JAVA 7 on your browser, and allow it to run if there is any prompt message. You can download it from `http://www.oracle.com/technetwork/java/javase/downloads/index.html`. If you cannot run the applet, refer to *Chapter 8, Troubleshooting on a Proxmox Cluster*, for troubleshooting.

Pay attention to OpenVZ-based VM; you will see that it cannot be accessed from the console because you have to configure *a getty service* inside the VM. So, we need to use another method for this purpose, for example, the OpenVZ management CLI:

1. Access your Proxmox console with the `root` account, as shown in the following screenshot:

```
login as: root
root@192.168.1.50's password:
Linux pve1 2.6.32-26-pve #1 SMP Mon Oct 14 08:22:20 CEST 2013 x86_64

The programs included with the Debian GNU/Linux system are free software;
the exact distribution terms for each program are described in the
individual files in /usr/share/doc/*/copyright.

Debian GNU/Linux comes with ABSOLUTELY NO WARRANTY, to the extent
permitted by applicable law.
Last login: Thu Feb 20 14:57:18 2014
root@pve1:~#
```

2. You can check the existing running OpenVZ containers with the `vzlist` command as shown in the following screenshot:

```
root@vmsrv01:~# vzlist
      CTID      NPROC STATUS    IP_ADDR         HOSTNAME
       100          4 running   192.168.1.10    myvm1.localdomain
```

3. Then, access it with `vzctl enter <CTID>`, for example, `vzctl enter 102`.

4. Create a new file under `/etc/init.d/tty.conf` with vi or any text editor you like.

5. Paste the following code in the `tty.conf` file:

```
# This service maintains agetty on tty1 from the point the
# system is started until it is shut down again.
start on stopped rc RUNLEVEL=[2345]
stop on runlevel [!2345]
respawn
exec /sbin/agetty -8 tty1 38400
```

6. Reboot the guest VM or type `start tty` to reboot.

Virtualization options in Proxmox VE

There are two types of virtualizations available in Proxmox: **OpenVZ** and **KVM**. What are the differences between them?

OpenVZ is an *operating-system-level virtualization* based on the GNU/Linux kernel and the host operation system. Theoretically, OpenVZ is not a type of virtualization but more like the *jail* concept in Linux. Since a *patched Linux kernel* is needed, only Linux guests can be created. All guests are called *containers* that share the same kernel and architecture as long as the host OS, while each container reserves a separate user space.

There is *no overhead* for OpenVZ as containers can call hardware resources directly. However, since all containers share the system kernel of the host OS, a system-related problem might appear during the host OS kernel upgrade. Besides, OpenVZ stores container files as normal files in the host OS, so it is not recommended to use OpenVZ if there are confidential files stored in the virtual machine. **Kernel-based Virtual Machine (KVM)** is basically a *hardware-assisted virtualization* with the modified Linux kernel *built with the KVM module*. KVM itself does not perform any emulation or virtualization. Instead, it simply exposes the /dev/kvm interface. QEMU is chosen as a software-based emulator to simulate hardware for the virtualized environment. The structure of KVM is shown as follows:

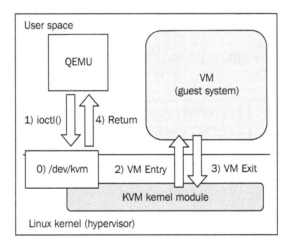

As we can see, overheads on frequent requests appear in QEMU-emulated devices. Thus, an improved version for KVM is published with *VirtIO drivers*. VirtIO creates a buffer for both the guest system and QEMU, which *speeds up the I/O performance and reduces the overhead*. To enjoy the performance burst, a VirtIO driver must be installed separately on each emulated hardware device. In the following diagram, we have demonstrated the new structure of the KVM machines with the VirtIO drivers installed:

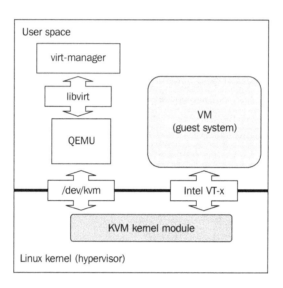

The following table shows the supported operating systems provided by OpenVZ and KVM:

Virtualization method	Supported operating system
OpenVZ	CentOS, Debian, Fedora, Scientific Linux, SUSE, and Ubuntu
KVM	FreeBSD, Windows Server 2000/XP/2003/2008, Windows 7/8, and all OS supported by OpenVZ

Virtual disk options under Proxmox VE

During the virtual machine creation, the following virtual disk options are available:

- **RAW**: This is a raw file format. The disk space is allocated during the creation and will use up the specified size. When compared with QCOW2, it gives a *better overall performance*.

- **QCOW2**: This is an enhanced version of QCOW, which offers a provisioning ability for disk storage used by QEMU. QCOW2 offers a capability to create multiple virtual machine snapshots compared to the older version. The following features are supported:
  - ° **Thin-provisioning**: During the disk creation, a file smaller than the specified size is created, and the specified size will be configured as the maximum size of the disk image. The file size will grow according to the usage inside the guest system; this is called thin-provisioning.
  - ° **Snapshot**: QCOW2 allows the user to create snapshots of the current system. With the use of the copy-on-write technology and a read-only base image, **differential backup** can be achieved.
  - ° **VMDK**: This file format for a disk image is used by VMware. The virtual disk file can be imported back to VMware Player, ESX, and ESXi. It also provides a thin-provisioning function such as QCOW2.

Introducing the OpenVZ template

Since the OpenVZ filesystem is only file-based, it is possible to pack the configurations and the disk image into a file for further deployment. We can create our own template file (which will be introduced in *Chapter 7, Disaster Recovery on a Proxmox VE Cluster*), or download the template file (also called a virtual appliance) via a web interface or from `http://download.proxmox.com/appliances/`.

Use these steps to download an OpenVZ template:

1. Log in to the web interface of Proxmox, and find **local storage** from the panel on the left-hand side.

2. Click on the **Content** tab and choose **Templates**, as shown in the following screenshot:

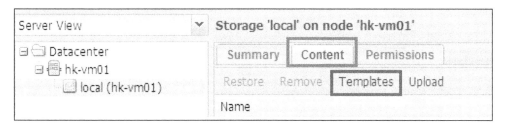

3. Next, we need to find a suitable template to download; for example, we can download a system with Drupal installed, as shown in the following screenshot:

Type	Package	Version	Description
Templates			✕
⊟ Section: www (7 Items)			
openvz	drupal	6.26-2	Drupal Content Management
openvz	wordpress	3.4.2-1	Wordpress

4. After we click on the **Download** button, the following progress window is shown along with the download details:

```
starting template download from: http://download.proxmox.com/appliances/www/debian-6.0-drupal_6.26-2_i386.tar.gz
target file: /var/lib/vz/template/cache/debian-6.0-drupal_6.26-2_i386.tar.gz
--2014-02-21 16:35:08--  http://download.proxmox.com/appliances/www/debian-6.0-drupal_6.26-2_i386.tar.gz
Resolving download.proxmox.com... 188.165.151.222
Connecting to download.proxmox.com|188.165.151.222|:80... connected.
HTTP request sent, awaiting response... 200 OK
Length: 181699863 (173M) [application/x-gzip]
Saving to: `/var/lib/vz/template/cache/debian-6.0-drupal_6.26-2_i386.tar.gz.tmp.622948'
               Progress bar          Completed / Speed / Estimated finish time
    OK ........ ........ ........ ........ ........ ........  1% 57.4K 50m38s
```

5. When the download completes, the template file is listed on the templates page, as shown in the following screenshot:

⊟ Templates (4 Items)		
centos-6-x86_64_minimal.tar.gz	tgz	167MB
debian-6.0-drupal_6.26-2_i386.tar.gz	tgz	173MB

Summary

In this chapter, we introduced the different modes of server virtualization, the reasons for using it, and how it actually works. We also caught a glimpse of the development on server virtualization by knowing the background technologies. Besides that, we learned the features and strengths of the different hypervisors on the market. Moreover, we went through some basic administration techniques of Proxmox, including the creation of virtual machines, importing OpenVZ templates, and viewing a guest system via the web console. Most importantly, we learned how to distinguish KVM and OpenVZ, which affects our decision during VM creation, for example, security versus performance.

In the next chapter, we are going to learn some concepts on high availability and the introduction of the Proxmox cluster.

2
Getting Started with a High Availability (HA) Environment

After *Chapter 1, Basic Concepts of a Proxmox Virtual Environment*, you might be excited to know how much more can we do with the help of Proxmox. Maybe you are already planning to virtualize your existing server with the help of Proxmox. Wait! Isn't it dangerous to centralize all servers in one physical machine? If you are an experienced system administrator, you must've been told to avoid a single point of failure; you have to minimize the number of services on a physical machine. We are now violating this rule; how should we solve this problem? In this chapter, we will cover the following topics:

- What is a high availability environment?
- Introducing a Proxmox VE cluster
- Hardware requirements for a Proxmox cluster
- How does Proxmox provide HA capacity?

What is a high availability (HA) environment?

If there is a single point of failure, can we simply add another identical server to solve it? The answer to this question is not as simple as a yes or a no. Even if we install the same software on two identical machines, how can we synchronize the data between them? It is not ideal to copy new data to the backup server manually. That's why the HA environment was created.

What is availability?

What does availability mean? Let's take a look at the formula to calculate the availability; we need to divide the subtraction of **Downtime duration** (DD) from **Expected uptime** (EU) with **Expected uptime** (EU) and then multiply it by 100. Availability is expressed as a percentage of uptime in a year. The formula is as follows:

$$\text{Availability } (\%) = \frac{\text{Expected uptime}\,(EU) - \text{Downtime duration}\,(DD)}{\text{Expected uptime}\,(EU)} \times 10$$

The terms used in the formula are explained as follows:

*   **Downtime duration (DD)**: This refers to the number of hours for which the system is unavailable
*   **Expected uptime (EU)**: This refers to the expected system availability; normally, we expect the system to be available for 365 x 24 x 7 hours

For example, if there are 100, 200, and 300 downtimes a month for a server and each downtime lasts for 4 hours, we will have following availability numbers:

Duration of downtime	Expected uptime (1 year)	Availability
100 x 4 = 400 hours	8760 hours	95%
200 x 4 = 800 hours	8760 hours	91%
300 x 4 = 1200 hours	8760 hours	86%

There are two types of downtime: *scheduled downtime* and *unscheduled downtime*. They are explained as follows:

*   **Scheduled downtime**: Traditionally, we have to make rooms for server package updates, hardware upgrades, configuration modifications, and so on. This type of downtime is inevitable, which should be a harmless, and it increases the stability and functionality of the server. Such downtime is under control, and the duration should be relatively short. The downtime is explained in the following diagram:

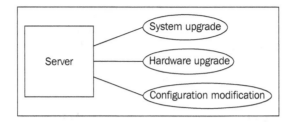

- **Unscheduled downtime**: This type of downtime includes hardware failures, software faults, human errors, and others. The duration of unscheduled downtime is unknown, but in general, it is much more than a scheduled one. Each unscheduled downtime should be taken into serious concern and should be avoided. This downtime is explained more clearly in the following diagram:

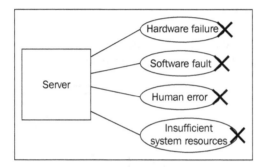

Negative effects of system downtime

We have gone through planned and unplanned downtime, and we all know that downtime is a bad thing. What are the problems caused because of downtime? Let's have a look:

- **Loss of customer trust**: This will have a huge impact if your application is an online buying platform. When a user tries to pay for the products or services they have selected, the system responds with an error page or, even worse, a white screen. If you were the customer, would you still trust this platform as a reliable one? I think the answer is no. Customers tend to share bad experiences with friends, and thus, a company's reputation will get damaged.

- **System recovery**: At the backend, quite a bit of system recovery and some troubleshooting tasks are required. Sometimes, we have to wait for support from the vendor, and they might not have essential service parts (this happens mostly for older systems). If this is the case, the repairing time will be longer than normal while you are still paying the rack rental fee to the data center, thus incurring a loss.

- **Reduction in the productivity of the internal staff**: If the affected server contains an internal system, the daily operation of the staff is affected. For example, when it is a CRM system, the sales staff cannot load customer information to process. When it is a financial system, the accountant cannot send and receive money from banks and the customers.

Strategies to achieve High Availability (HA)

Now, come back to the word, *High Availability*. HA means that we have to build an infrastructure to escape from these downtimes. We have the following strategies to achieve HA:

- **Load balancing**: If the downtime is caused by insufficient system resources, adding a new server with a *load balancer* in between could increase the level of availability. The advantage of load balancing is that it does not require identical server machines. With the help of this technique, a server with a 90 percent system load can be reduced to a 50 percent system load. Thus, it helps reduce the chance of a system failure due to insufficient resources.

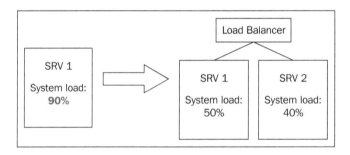

There are **software-based (SW-based)** and **hardware-based (HW-based)** load balancers; the main difference between them is that the SW-based load balancer requires user installation, while the hardware-based load balancer is ready to use when it is delivered. The differences are given in the following table:

Type	Product	Configuration difficulty	Price
Reverse proxy	Nginx, Squid	Medium	Low
SW-based load balancer	HAProxy, Zen load balancer	High	Low
HW-based load balancer	F5 Big-IP® Local Traffic Manager	Low	High

- **Failover**: This is similar to load balancing but requires an identical server machine as a standby. Imagine that we have two identical servers; there is a heartbeat between the two servers to identify whether any one of the systems have failed or not. The following points explain how it works:

  ° Initially there is a *heartbeat* signal in between SRV1 and SRV2, and **Server2 (SRV2)** is in the *standby* state

  ° When **Server1 (SRV1)** fails, the heartbeat signal from SRV1 is missing, and it notifies SRV2

  ° SRV2 takes over SRV1's responsibility and makes it active

This has been explained in the following diagram:

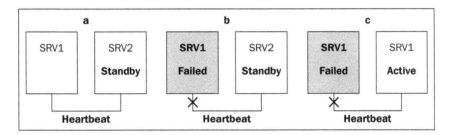

- **Heartbeat**: This is a key term for a HA environment. It is used to check the availability of each cluster member node and perform certain actions according to the system state changes. There are a few types of operations needed to detect such a problem. For example, we can set up the following two conditions with heartbeat:

  ° **The first condition**: UDP packets are sent between SRV1 and SRV2 in order to test the current status of SRV1. If SRV1 becomes unavailable, the heartbeat will return a failed result and turn on the running services of SRV1 on SRV2. This test is used to check whether the connection between SRV1 and SRV2 is working properly.

  ° **The second condition**: A ping operation takes place from both SRV1 and SRV2 to an external IP address. This will guarantee that the connection of both the servers to an outside network is working properly. If one of the conditions shows a false status, the corresponding server node will be either shut down or disconnected, and it relocates the virtual machines to the other node.

For more details on the configuration we used, refer to *Chapter 4, Configuring a Proxmox VE Cluster*.

* **Redundancy**: Have you noticed that there is a problem with the failover method? What if there is a connection problem between SRV1 and SRV2? Redundancy is an improved version of the single failover method; failover is not only applied at the server level but also at the infrastructure level. Here, we have a simple diagram for your understanding:

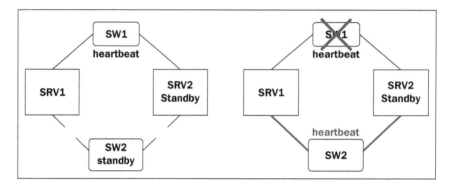

There is a **standby switch (SW2)** in between two servers. When the **production switch (SW1)** fails, **SRV1** and **SRV2** will choose **SW2** as the new path to send the heartbeat signals. So, we won't disable a server node by mistake. What will happen if we disabled a server node in a wrong way?

For example, we have a healthy server node, SRV1, but heartbeat service treated it as failed due to the network delay. Thus, all services that are running under SRV1 will be activated in SRV2. To avoid data corruption caused by multiple accesses at both nodes, SRV1 will be disabled. In this case, the network card will be disabled to avoid access to the shared storage. Therefore, we need to have a network interface for management use and will not join the cluster operation for manual recovery.

To reach a high level of availability, we have to choose *redundancy* mode from the strategies mentioned.

Introducing a Proxmox VE cluster

Now, we have some idea about how to measure the availability level for a server; increasing the availability is very important for us. Is it possible for Proxmox to deal with this task? Yes, of course, but it is only available in cluster mode. The basic difference between single instance versus clusters under Proxmox is as follows:

Product	Proxmox VE	Proxmox VE Cluster
Number of nodes	1	2 (minimum)
Quorum disk	No	Yes
Storage	Local	Shared
HA	No	Yes

Unlike running with a single Proxmox instance, we need to provide shared storage for the cluster to keep the data of virtual machines. In our configuration, we would like to use a package called DRBD, which allows us to use local storage from both servers to form a shared RAID 1 storage. The data synchronization will automatically be managed by the DRBD package. So, we don't need to purchase additional network storage for our testing.

Introduction to DRBD

DRBD is a short form for **Distributed Replicated Block Device**; it is intended to be used under a HA environment. DRBD provides high availability by mirroring the existing system to another machine, including the disk storage, network card status, and services that run under the existing system. So, if the existing system is out of service, we can instantly switch to the backup system to avoid service interruption. This has been explained in the following diagram:

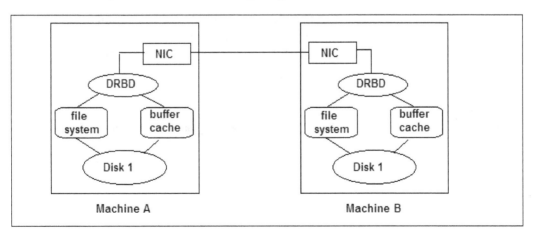

In our case, we would like to focus on the data synchronization on the local storage. For more details on the configuration, refer to *Chapter 4, Configuring a Proxmox VE Cluster*.

Besides HA, there are a few more functions provided by the Proxmox cluster mode, but the most important one is *live migration*. Unlike normal migration, in a Proxmox cluster, migration can be accomplished without shutting down the virtual machine. Such an approach is called **live migration**, which greatly reduces the downtime of each virtual machine.

Explaining live migration

Live migration can be divided into two techniques: **pre-copy memory migration** for the *KVM-based VM* and **post-copy memory migration** for the *OpenVZ-based VM*. The difference between pre-copy and post-copy is that pre-copy *can recover migration* error while post-copy cannot. Let's see how live migration works in the OpenVZ-based VM first.

Introducing the post-copy memory migration

When post-copy memory migration takes place, the following steps are performed:

1. Data in the OpenVZ container is copied to the destination server (**SRV2**).

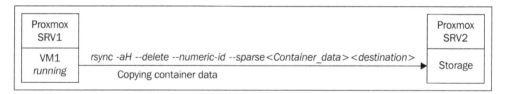

2. After that, the original VM (**VM1**) is suspended, and a minimal set of system resources, including CPU, registers, and non-paging memory, is delivered to the destination server (**SRV2**); this process is called **pre-paging**.

3. **VM1** is resumed at **SRV2**; meanwhile, **VM1** at **SRV1** will actively push the remaining memory pages to **SRV2**.

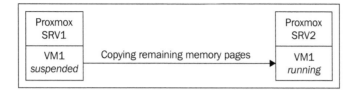

When the new **VM1** accesses the memory pages, a page fault is generated. This will then be redirected back to **VM1** at **SRV1** to solve the problem. Such redirection is defined as a network fault, which degrades system performance.

Post-copy memory migration can be used in OpenVZ-based virtual machines, because the data content of the VM is stored under files and folders. So, we can simply copy the data via the SSH tunnel in a local network, which is supposed to be very fast. Next, let's check out how *pre-copy memory migration* works.

Introducing the pre-copy memory migration

Under KVM, we have a different type of migration process; this is called pre-copy memory migration. During the pre-copy memory migration, **warm-up phase** and **stop-and-copy phase** are executed. The following are the steps that occur in the pre-copy memory migration:

1. In the *warm-up phase*, Proxmox attempts to copy all memory pages from source to destination while the virtual machine is *still running*.

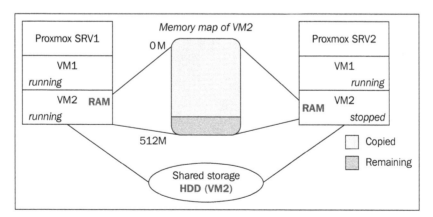

2. If there is any change in the source memory pages, the corresponding memory pages on the target machine are marked as *dirty*. After we have copied the memory pages from the source machine, the memory pages marked as *dirty* are recopied to the destination until the rate of the recopied pages is larger than the rate of dirty pages to make sure only minor changes are there.

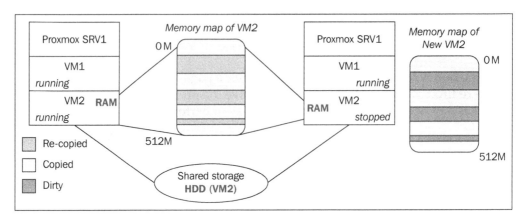

3. When the rate of dirty pages is less than that of recopied pages, the *warm-up* phase ends and the *stop-and-copy phase* starts. The original **VM2** will be stopped, and the remaining dirty pages will be copied to destination Proxmox. This is actual *downtime* for **VM2**; it ranges from milliseconds to seconds.

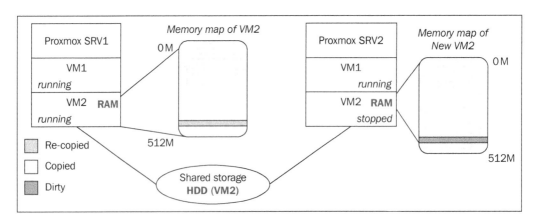

4. Having copied all the dirty pages from the original **VM2**, **VM2** will be resumed at the target Proxmox machine.

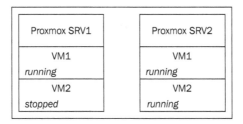

System requirements for the Proxmox cluster

So, we have talked so much about the Proxmox cluster. To use this mode, we have to first prepare at least two machines that are installed with Proxmox VE. If we want to have a basic testing platform, what would be the minimum requirement for our machines?

The *minimum system requirements* as listed on the Proxmox website are as follows:

*   CPU: 64-bit (Intel EMT64 or AMD64)
*   Intel VT/AMD-V capable CPU/Mainboard (for KVM)
*   Minimum 1 GB RAM
*   Hard drive
*   One NIC

However, I would recommend that you have at least *2 GB* memory if you want to test online migration on the Windows platform.

For a production environment, the following hardware is suggested by Proxmox:

*   CPU: The CPU must support 64-bit (Intel EMT64 or AMD64), *multicore* CPU is recommended, and Intel VT/AMD-V capable CPU/mainboard is required (for KVM support)
*   8 GB RAM is good; the more the better
*   *Hardware RAID with* **battery backup unit** (**BBU**) or flash-based protection (software RAID is not officially supported by Proxmox, but it is possible)
*   Fast hard drives, such as SAS drives with a 15k rpm will give the best results, *RAID 10*
*   At least two NIC's per Proxmox server

- In cluster mode, we need at least *two physical servers* that meet the requirements mentioned earlier, a network to connect both of them, and shared storage to keep virtual disk data

No matter whether you go for the minimum or suggested system requirements, you also need to prepare the things mentioned in the following points:

- At least one multicast capable switch is needed.
- Shared storage that is accessible by both Proxmox servers is needed as a quorum disk *if we have only two server nodes*. A quorum disk is used to add an extra vote inside the cluster. More details on this will be introduced in *Chapter 4, Configuring a Proxmox VE Cluster*.
- Fencing devices are required on *all* server nodes; it can be a network-based or power-based server node. More details on this will be introduced in *Chapter 3, Key Components for Building a Proxmox VE Cluster*.

Personally, I would suggest that you build your own Proxmox cluster with three or more machines. It would reduce the possibility of getting errors with the cluster itself, especially the problem caused by not having enough votes for cluster operation; this will block any cluster-related activity. However, for practice, I will go through a two-node cluster with you in the upcoming chapters. In the next section, I would like to show you some concepts on RAID requirement.

Describing the requirements for RAID

As you might know, there is software RAID and hardware RAID. As Proxmox recommends hardware RAID first, we focus only on it. In a RAID operation, there are different levels, including RAID 0 and RAID 1, and the one recommended by Proxmox, RAID 10. Let's see the difference.

The RAID 0 operation

Under RAID level 0, we have to use at least two hard disks to form a group. After joining them up, the read performance is theoretically increased by n times (two times in our case), because I/O requests are responded to by all hard disks. However, if any one of the hard disks (**HDD1**) fails, the whole disk group (**RAID 0**) will fail, as shown in the following diagram:

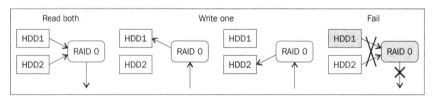

The RAID 1 operation

As there is no fault tolerance in RAID level 0, it is not suitable for production use. Therefore, RAID level 1 is introduced; this could increase the availability. As the data is written to all hard disks, *it can still be read even if there is only one workable hard disk*. The disadvantage of RAID 1 is that the performance of the write operation is reduced. RAID 1 is explained in the following diagram:

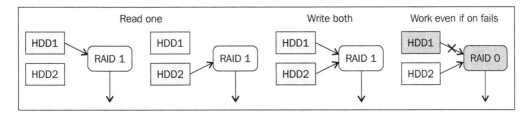

The RAID 10 operation

Actually, both RAID 0 and RAID 1 have their own advantages and disadvantages. What if we combine them together? This is where RAID 10 appears. In RAID 10, we need at least *four hard disks*. We first form a RAID 1 volume from two hard disks and then we have two RAID 1 volumes. Then, we form a RAID 0 volume by combining the RAID 1 volumes. So, we can enjoy the performance burst when reading from two RAID 1 volumes (one hard disk is read from each RAID 1 volume). During the write operation, only one RAID 1 volume is used. Therefore, the performance of the write operation will not decrease. RAID 10 is explained in the following diagram:

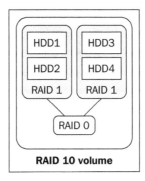

Now we will learn about *battery backup unit* and *flash-based protection*:

- **Battery backup unit (BBU)**: The hardware RAID controller provides *integrated caches* to increase the I/O performance. However, it is rather dangerous for data integrity because cache is a temporary storage and the data can be lost if case of a power loss occurs. BBU will *provide power* to the cache memory if a power loss occurs to keep the integrity of the data intact. After the power is restored, the data writes back to the permanent storage. Here is how it works:

  1. First, data is stored in the cache memory of the RAID controller, and then writes the data to the hard disk as the permanent source of storage

  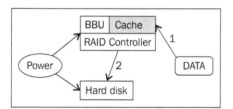

  2. When a power loss occurs, the hard disk is not usable, and the data (**data1**, **data2**, and **data3**) is stored in the cache memory.

  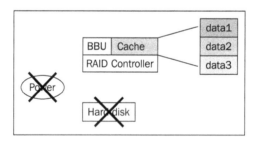

  3. When the power is restored, **data1**, **data2**, and **data3** are written back to the hard disk.

  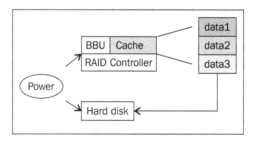

- **Flash-based protection**: In this mode, the cache is stored in a solid state, that is, in NAND flash memory instead of cache memory. NAND flash memory is a permanent storage memory, which is therefore resistant in the case of a power loss.

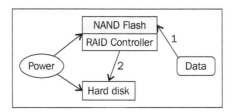

In the next section, I will discuss how Proxmox provides HA capability under cluster mode with two server nodes.

HA capability for Proxmox with a two-node cluster

In this section, I will show you how a Proxmox cluster helps us in enhancing the system availability. Assume that we are building a cluster with two active member nodes, which means virtual machines are running on both the server nodes. Let's take a look at the following structure:

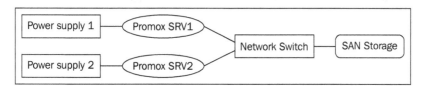

As we mentioned in the section on *system requirements*, we need at least two physical servers connected with a network switch, and we need SAN storage to save virtual disk images. This is the minimal requirement to build a cluster. With this set of hardware, we can successfully install Proxmox in cluster mode. However, is it built with *high* availability? Unfortunately, it is not; let's see what happens when we cannot connect our network switch due to misconfiguration or hardware problems:

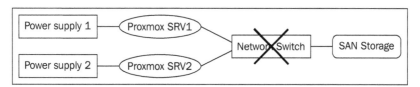

Right now, both servers think that the other side is out of service, as **SRV1** and **SRV2** cannot contact each other. What will they do? They will try to migrate the virtual machines from the SAN storage, but they can't. Therefore, the cluster is down. How about we add an extra network switch?

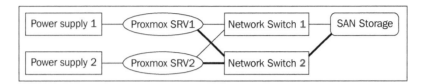

We found that even if one network switch is broken down, there is still another backup path that ensures the communication between devices. This is a setting for a *redundant network* that archives HA. However, a similar problem occurs in the SAN storage, as shown in the following diagram:

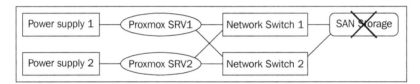

Is there any need to purchase a SAN storage for our cluster? Not really, because SAN storage is quite expensive, and the synchronization between multiple SAN storages is another problem. To solve this, DRBD is used as a cheaper solution.

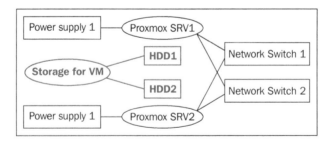

In this model, the local storage of **SRV1** and **SRV2** is used to form a mirrored network storage with the help of DRDB. As Proxmox does not offer a solution for us to easily build shared storage between servers, DRDB is being used in our demonstration so that we don't have to purchase additional storage hardware to store the virtual machine data. I would suggest that you use the DRBD storage for testing purposes, but for the production platform, it would be better to have separate shared storage. DRBD, in our case, is used to synchronize the content of **HDD1** and **HDD2** via the network; therefore, the content inside both the hard disks is identical. As a result, a disk-level redundancy is achieved.

What will happen if there is problem in the Proxmox server? A new term called **fencing** is introduced to mark the problematic server as unreachable and to power it off. We will discuss this in more detail in *Chapter 3*, *Key Components for Building a Proxmox VE Cluster*.

The Proxmox Cluster file system (pmxcfs)

Are you curious to know how to manage multiple configuration files in the Proxmox cluster mode? **Proxmox Cluster file system** (**pmxcfs**) is a built-in function that is provided with a Proxmox cluster to synchronize configuration files between cluster member nodes. It is an essential component for a Proxmox cluster; it acts as version control on configuration files, including cluster configuration, the virtual machine configuration, and so on. It basically is a database-driven filesystem to store configuration files for all the host servers and replicate them in real time on all the host nodes, using *corosync*. The underlying filesystem is created by FUSE, with a maximum size of 30 MB. The main concepts of this filesystem are as follows:

- **FUSE**: This is a short form for **Filesystem in Userspace** (**FUSE**). It allows users to define their own device under their own userspace. With the use of FUSE, we don't have to worry if the system crashes due to filesystem misconfiguration, because FUSE is not linked to the system kernel.

- **Corosync**: This is a short form for **Corosync Cluster Engine**, a group communication system that allows clients to communicate with each other.

The following diagram shows the structure of the Proxmox cluster filesystem:

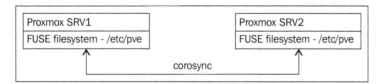

Under the filesystem, there are some files we might be interested in:

- `cluster.conf`: This is the cluster configuration file

- `nodes/${NAME}/qemu-server/${VMID}.conf`: This file contains the KVM configuration data

- `nodes/${NAME}/openvz/${VEID}.conf`: This file contains the OpenVZ configuration data

Summary

In this chapter, we talked about the types of system downtime and their impact and how to measure and increase the level of availability. One of the most important features, live migration, was also explained briefly. Finally, we went through the cluster filesystem in order to know how Proxmox maintains its configuration files. In the next chapter, we will talk about the key components that will be used when we build the cluster, including the *DRDB device*, *reliable network*, and a *fencing device*.

3
Key Components for Building a Proxmox VE Cluster

Now, we are going to learn about the components needed to build a reliable cluster with Proxmox VE. Let's have an overview of the HA environment. We require a shared storage to save system and user data for the VM, a reliable network with redundancy, multiple physical servers, and a fencing device to prevent multiple access to the VM. The topics included in this chapter are:

- An introduction to the storage options supported by Proxmox
- An introduction to the requirements for a reliable network
- An introduction to fencing devices
- An introduction to quorum disks

Key component 1 – shared storage

In order to ensure HA, we must not have a single point of failure, which means each virtual machine should be able to be accessed by multiple Proxmox servers. If there is one failed Proxmox server, there should be another server to handle the associated VM. Therefore, we should not store our VMs in local storage; we should store them on shared storage. In a modern technology environment, network storage is commonly used as shared storage, which has led to the coining of the terms, **storage area network (SAN)** and **network-attached storage (NAS)**.

Characteristics of SAN and NAS

Storage area network (SAN) is mounted as *block-level* storage. The commonly used protocols to mount a SAN device are *iSCSI* and *fibre channel*. When the storage is mounted, it appears as a local disk inside the system, allowing the operating system to manage its filesystem. Based on this characteristic, the storage is expected to be permanently attached to the operating system. The following is the output of disk management under the Windows platform, after we have mounted a hard disk using iSCSI:

```
Disk /dev/sdf: 160.0 GB, 160040803840 bytes
255 heads, 63 sectors/track, 19457 cylinders, total 312579695 sectors
Units = sectors of 1 * 512 = 512 bytes
Sector size (logical/physical): 512 bytes / 512 bytes
I/O size (minimum/optimal): 512 bytes / 512 bytes
Disk identifier: 0x0003ee9f
```

Network-attached storage (NAS), on the other hand, is provided as *file-level* storage. The storage is shared via the **SMB** or **NFS** protocol. As it is file-level storage, separate permission settings can be applied to different files and directories. Unlike the mounted hard disk described earlier, the storage via the SMB or NFS protocol is added as a mount point, and it can be easily removed from system using the umount command. The following example shows how NAS shares its storage:

```
Filesystem            Size  Used Avail Use% Mounted on
//192.168.1.50/myshare   160G  105G  55G  65% /myshare
```

Basically, the data inside a VM can be stored in both SAN and NAS. However, for better performance and stability, it is suggested that you store data in something similar to SAN.

Available storage options in Proxmox

Apart from the types of storage mentioned earlier, Proxmox also supports distributed filesystem. Hence, we have the following storage options available in Proxmox:

- **directory**
- **logical volume manager (LVM)**
- **iSCSI target**
- **NFS share**
- **Gluster filesystem**
- **Ceph** (marked as **RBD** in Proxmox)

Storage option 1 – storage over iSCSI

To build a HA environment, it is not enough to share the hard disk from network storage under iSCSI; we have to build a RAID volume as a shared storage under the iSCSI server. The following is a simple diagram that shows the structure of our iSCSI disk:

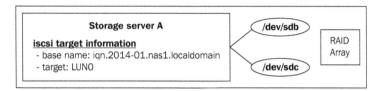

The base name format is predefined in RFC3721, and we cannot simply type whatever we want. Let's use this sample for explanation. The full target name for **Storage server A** is **iqn.2014-01.nas1.localdomain:disk0**.

The storage server's naming convention has been explained in the following points:

- **Iqn**: This indicates that it is an iSCSI device
- **2014-01**: This indicates the date when we this iSCSI volume storage was created
- **nas1.localdomain**: This indicates a reversed DNS name for storage server A
- **disk0**: This is the storage name; we can change it by adding the disk type and who creates it

In this storage option, we can have shared storage on multiple Proxmox servers, but we cannot ensure that the storage is limited to single access. To solve this problem, we have to build a cluster-based filesystem, for example, the LVM volume. The following diagram shows the possible settings for the clustered-LVM volume formed with iSCSI devices:

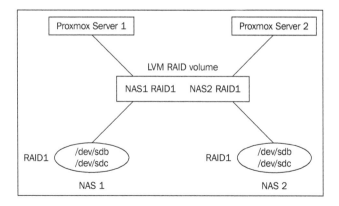

An explanation of the Logical Volume Manager (LVM)

Unlike building a local RAID 1 device using the `mdadm` command, we need to form a volume for the LVM with a dedicated local disk in multiple servers. LVM is used to simplify the disk management process of large hard disks. By adding an abstraction layer, users are able to add/replace their hard disks without downtime in combination with *hot swapping*. Besides, users are able to add/remove/resize their LVM volumes or even create a RAID volume easily. The structure of a LVM is shown in the following diagram:

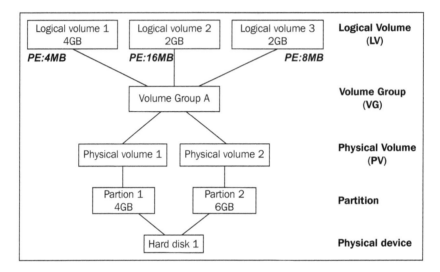

The following steps will help you create a volume for the LVM with the configuration shown in the preceding diagram:

1. First, let's create *partitions* of the hard disk (**Hard disk 1**) using the `fdisk` command. The system IDs for the partitions are marked as `8E` (`LVM`) during the creation process.

2. The created partitions, **partition 1** and **partition 2**, will be further converted to **Physical Volume (PV)**.

3. Multiple PVs can be gathered to form **Volume Group (VG) A**.

4. Each **Logical Volume (LV)** that lies in a **logical group (LG)** can be formatted to a filesystem such as EXT3/4, NTFS, and so on. At this point, we can define the **physical extents (PE)** (the default size is 4 MB each), which is similar to the *block size* that is used when we format a physical disk.

What if we want to increase the size of the logical volume? It is not as easy as adding a new hard drive. The following steps only show you how to increase the size of a logical group and logical volumes. However, these steps will not cover the steps to handle any resizing problem with the filesystem that we might face during the process. We add 10 GB extra space to all the logical volumes, and the new structure after the volume expansion is shown in the following diagram:

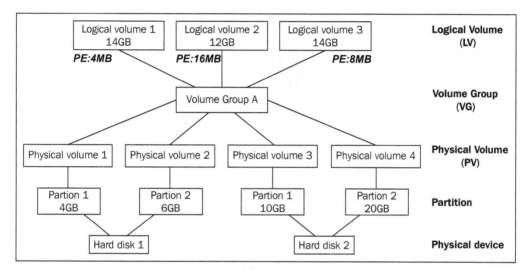

To add new volumes to the existing LVM volume group, follow these steps:

1. First, we add another hard disk, **Hard disk 2**, into the system and create corresponding PVs as we did earlier.

2. We then add **Physical volume 3** and **Physical volume 4** to **Volume Group A** using the `vgextend` command.

3. Finally, we make use of the `lvresize` command to resize the existing LVs.

As you can see, we can dynamically allocate disk space in a LVM, but we cannot add an LVM partition to an iSCSI Logical Unit Number (LUN) or DRBD once it is created. In such a configuration, the LVM volume is shared by the DRBD package. Also, if we have mounted the LVM storage as a local directory in Proxmox, we will not only be able to store the data inside the VM, but also inside the ISO files, OS templates, and the OpenVZ containers. A demonstration of how to use an LVM over iSCSI as storage will be covered in *Chapter 4, Configuring a Proxmox VE Cluster*.

Storage option 2 – a distributed replicated block device (DRBD)

In a DRBD structure, the primary and secondary nodes are connected via a network, and every single update request on the primary node is synchronized with the secondary node via network interface cards. As the data is being synchronized, identical server specifications must be reached. With such a structure, we are able to restart "dead" VMs from another server, as shown in the following diagram:

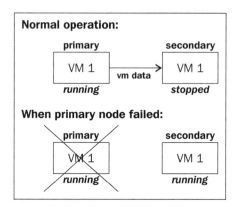

Unfortunately, the service restoration process is not automatic, and manual operation is needed. It is not good news for us because it is difficult for us to monitor the system on a 24 x 7 basis. To overcome this, fencing devices are used to finish the tasks for us. In the upcoming chapters, we will talk more about the structure and concept of fencing devices and how they help us in the production environment.

Storage option 3 – the Gluster filesystem

GlusterFS is a **distributed filesystem** that runs on the server-client architecture. It makes use of the native Gluster protocol, but can also be seen as an NFS share or even work as an object storage (Amazon S3-like networked key-value storage) with GlusterFS UFO.

The base components of Gluster volumes are bricks, which are built with directories. More information will be available in *Chapter 4, Configuring a Proxmox VE Cluster*.

By exporting the disk drives to Gluster servers, Gluster client is able to *create virtual volumes* from multiple remote servers with petabytes (*1 PB = 1000 TB = 1000000 GB*) of storage. Similar to LVM over iSCSI, the storage is scalable when new disk drives are available. GlusterFS can be further configured to store files in replication or strip form.

A better approach to Gluster over LVM with iSCSI is its **auto healing** function. With auto healing, the Gluster client will still be able to read/write files even if one Gluster server has failed; this is similar to what **RAID 1** offered. Let's read more on how the Gluster filesystem handles server failure:

1. Initially, we require at least two storage servers installed with the Gluster server package in order to enjoy the functionality of auto healing. On the client side, we configured it to use **Replicate mode** and mount the filesystem to /glusterfs, as shown in the following diagram:

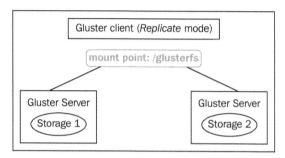

2. The file content will be stored in both the storages in this mode, as shown in the following diagram:

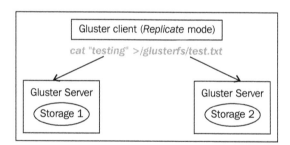

3. If **Storage 1** fails, the Gluster client will redirect the request to **Storage 2**, as shown in the following diagram:

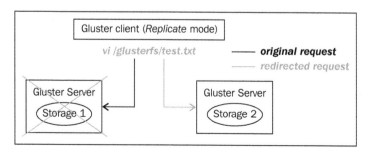

4. When **Storage 1** becomes available, the updated content will be synchronized with **Storage 2**. Therefore, the client will not notice if there is a server failure. This is shown in the following diagram:

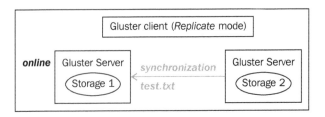

Thus, the Gluster filesystem can provide HA if we use replication mode. For performance, we can distribute the file to more servers, as shown in the following diagram:

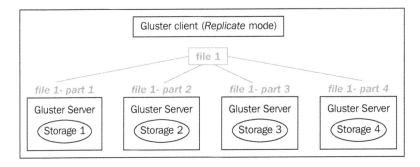

In this architecture, each file is divided into different pieces that are stored in separate storages. Such an approach *reduces the chances of reaching the I/O limit* on a single storage during the write operation and *boosts up the read performance* by reading from multiple storage sources, but a high-speed network is required to avoid reaching the I/O limit under the network environment.

Storage option 4 – the Ceph filesystem

Ceph is also a *distributed filesystem* that provides petabyte-level storage but is more focused on eliminating a single point of failure. To ensure HA, replicas are created on other storage nodes. Ceph was developed based on the concepts of **RADOS (Reliable Autonomic Distributed Object Store)**, with different accessing methods provided:

Accessing method	Support platforms	Usage
Library packages	C, C++, JAVA, Python, Ruby, and PHP	Programming
RADOS gateway	Amazon S3 and Swift	Cloud platform

Accessing method	Support platforms	Usage
RBD	KVM	Virtualization
CEPH filesystem	Linux kernel and FUSE	Filesystem

Under Ceph, everything is stored in the form of an object, which is why Ceph is also called *object storage cluster*. To make sure that the objects are replicated correctly, multiple objects will be mapped to the **Placement Group** (**PG**). Regarding the server components, the storage node is called the **Ceph object storage devices** (**OSD**) **daemon**, and **Ceph monitors** maintain a master copy of the *cluster map*. Here is the explanation of these:

- **Object**: This is the *smallest unit* in the Ceph storage. As the data is stored in a flat namespace, each object is stored with an identifier (**UUID**).

- **Placement Group**: This is a series of objects that are grouped together and replicated to multiple OSDs based on PG. We prefer using PG over objects, because tracking on a per-object basis is *computationally expensive*. The manipulation of PG effectively *reduces* the number of processes and the per-object metadata to be tracked during a data read/write operation. The following formula is used to calculate the number of PGs we need:

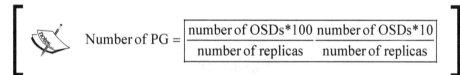

$$\text{Number of PG} = \boxed{\frac{\text{number of OSDs} * 100}{\text{number of replicas}} \quad \frac{\text{number of OSDs} * 10}{\text{number of replicas}}}$$

- **Pool**: This is formed by multiple PGs, and it allows the system administrators to configure settings such as *number of replicas per object*, number of placement groups per OSD, defining the CRUSH rule, and creating snapshots and setting ownership. To store data inside a pool, an authorized user account is needed. The default pools include data, metadata, and RBD.

- **Ceph OSD daemon**: This daemon must be run to establish a client connection. After the OSD is mounted, the client can use it as if they are using their own local hard drives. Each OSD should be associated with hard drives that enable the RAID arrays or LVM to enhance performance.

- **Ceph monitor daemon**: This daemon is used to provide a recent copy of a *cluster map*, including information for the Ceph monitor, OSD, PG, the CRUSH map, and MD5 map.

The following screenshot is an example of how an OSD daemon stores a file:

ID	Binary Data	Metadata	
1234	0101010101010100110101010010 0101100001010100110101010010 0101100001010100110101010010	name1 name2 nameN	value1 value2 valueN

It's quite difficult to get familiar with wordings, so I have prepared the following simple diagram that demonstrates the concepts for you:

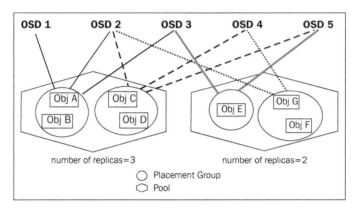

From the diagram, **Obj A** and **Obj B** belong to one **PG** just as **Obj C** and **Obj D** belong to one **PG**. **Obj E** is stored in a single **PG,** while **Obj G** and **Obj F** are in the same **PG**. **Obj A** to **Obj D** are stored in **Pool 1**, while **Obj E** to **Obj F** are stored in **Pool 2**.

As the number of replicas in **Pool 1** is set to three, the placement group that contains **Obj A** and **Obj B** are replicated through **OSD 1**, **OSD 2**, and **OSD 3**. Although **Obj C** and **Obj D** are stored in the same pool of **Obj A** and **Obj B**, they stored in different OSDs.

An important concept in Ceph is the **cluster map**; it includes most of the Ceph-related information, as explained in the following points:

- **Monitor map**: This map contains the cluster FSID, the position, name address, and port of each monitor.

- **OSD map**: This map contains the cluster FSID, a list of pool, replica sizes, PG numbers, and a list of OSDs and their statuses.

- **PG map**: This map contains PG version, the last OSD map epoch (that is version), its timestamp, and details on each placement group.

- **CRUSH map**: This map contains a list of storage devices and the rules to traverse the filesystem when storing data. The **CRUSH algorithm** makes use of this map to calculate which OSD should be used by clients to store data.

- **MDS map**: Here, MDS stands for metadata server. MDS is used to store the entire filesystem's metadata (directories, file ownership, access modes, and so on) when using the Ceph filesystem, and it is deployed with a Ceph storage cluster. Also, a list of metadata servers and their statuses are stored in the MDS map.

Notice that a functional Ceph requires a minimal system with *one Ceph monitor* and *two OSDs* for data replication, as shown in the following diagram. We will also demonstrate how to work with a Ceph storage cluster in the next chapter.

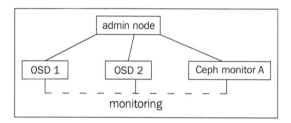

Comparing the types of file storage supported by Proxmox

We have understood the storage options that are supported by Proxmox, but what are the differences between them? Let's take a look at these differences. The following are the advantages of an iSCSI-based storage option:

- It allows a user to reserve the whole hard disk on remote storage

- It provides the authentication ability using the CHAP protocol

- In this, the storage can be restricted to allow access to the clients in a specific network

- With multiple LUNs, clients can access different disk arrays from remote storage

- This is available for both Windows and Linux platforms

The following are the disadvantages of an iSCSI-based storage option:

- The user permissions cannot be assigned to a single storage
- It has no data integrity without further settings (for example, RAID, and ZFS)
- The I/O performance is slower than it is in a local storage option
- Dedicated network storage is needed
- The scalability of this type of disk storage is limited

The following are the advantages of DRBD:

- User permissions can be applied to this type of storage, because it is mounted as a directory
- Data integrity is ensured due to live data synchronization
- No extra storage is needed, because local storage is used

The following are the disadvantages of DRBD:

- As it is based on two nodes, a situation called split-brain might take place; this causes the storage to become unavailable. Manual recovery is needed.
- The initialization process is slow because it needs to copy every single block from the master disk.

The following are the advantages of GlusterFS:

- Data integrity is ensured with multiple configured nodes
- Metadata can be stored in a **solid-state drive** (**SSD**) to increase the performance
- Automatic data recovery called auto healing is available on a Gluster-based volume
- High scalability can be achieved on a Gluster volume by adding new nodes

The following are the disadvantages of GlusterFS:

- Multiple TCP ports should be opened for Gluster traffic; firewall configuration is needed
- I/O performance is heavily related to network throughput; Gigabit Ethernet would be the minimum requirement, that is, high-level network switches are needed

The following are the advantages of CEPH:

- There's a built-in CEPH server for Proxmox; hence, it is easier to implement it
- Similar to GlusterFS, metadata can be stored in a SSD to increase the performance
- It has the ability of self-healing, which is provided by the CRUSH algorithm

The following are the disadvantages of CEPH:

- If the CEPH server service is running under a Proxmox host, system resources will be used by the storage
- Many new terms are associated with CEPH; you need to learn their basic concepts before migrating to CEPH

The following table compares the storage options supported by Proxmox:

Storage option	iSCSI	DRBD	GlusterFS	CEPH
Cost	Hardware-based NAS: High Software-based NAS: Low	Low	Medium	Medium
Difficulty on implementation	Easy	Easy	Medium	Easy (via GUI)
Data-protection level	No, provided by filesystem	Low (data synchronization)	High (file replica)	High (file replica)
Scalability	Low	Low	High	High

I have tested the performance of these storage options for two different scenarios: copying 1,000 small files (1 MB each) and copying one big file (1 GB). CEPH storage is not being tested because it is available for storing KVM images only and, by default, has no mount point option under Proxmox.

The following table has the performance benchmark results for small files:

Storage options	Local storage	DRBD	GlusterFS
CPU loading	25%	28%	25%
Memory usage	10 MB	10 MB	10 MB
Time taken	1 min 36 sec	1 min 31 sec	4 min 9 sec

The following table has the performance benchmark results for the large file:

Storage options	Local storage	DRBD	GlusterFS
CPU Loading	50%	50%	30%
Memory usage	10 MB	10 MB	10 MB
Time taken	1 min 25 sec	2 min 51 sec	3 min 3 sec

Based on the result, the performance of DRBD storage is almost the same as using local storage, but we can enjoy the advantage of having a network RAID 1 for storage. For GlusterFS, the performance is a little less than the others, but in the long term, I suggest using a cluster filesystem such as GlusterFS and CEPH in the production environment, because of the scalability and multiple replicas that are available, while DRBD would be a good storage option for a testing platform.

Key component 2 – reliable network

Based on our setting, almost all the components are running through the network. This means that a stable and fast network is essential. The best practice is to separate the network for data replication, storage, and management. So, what does a fast network mean? Only gigabit Ethernet or a faster version will be chosen; this means that all the servers should have gigabit Ethernet cards in a local area network connection. Besides, we need to measure the connection time between two nodes to ensure that the speed is optimal. Moreover, all of the running nodes should be in the same subnet to avoid the involvement of further routing processes.

The following screenshot is a simple ping test to measure the network latency on the network; pay attention to the time column, which should never be longer than *1 ms*:

```
root@vm01:~# ping 192.168.1.1
PING 192.168.1.1 (192.168.1.1) 56(84) bytes of data.
64 bytes from 192.168.1.1: icmp_req=1 ttl=64 time=0.339 ms
64 bytes from 192.168.1.1: icmp_req=2 ttl=64 time=0.303 ms
64 bytes from 192.168.1.1: icmp_req=3 ttl=64 time=0.293 ms
64 bytes from 192.168.1.1: icmp_req=4 ttl=64 time=0.296 ms
```

To check whether a gigabit Ethernet card has been loaded, the `lshw` command can be used. However, it is not a built-in command; we have to install it first. Type the following command in the terminal to install it:

```
sudo apt-get install lshw
```

Then, issue the `lshw | grep Ethernet` command; you will see the following output:

```
root@vm01:~# lshw | grep Ethernet
              description: Ethernet interface
              product: RTL8111/8168B PCI Express Gigabit Ethernet controller
```

For network stability, we have to construct a network with HA, as shown in the following diagram:

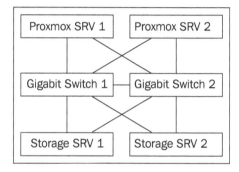

Key component 3 – a fencing device

So, we have talked about the two key components of a Proxmox HA cluster; they are the storage devices and reliable network. Do you remember that I mentioned a fencing device when I introduced DRBD? Do you know what a fencing device is and how it works? We'll learn more about this in the following section.

What is a fencing device?

A fencing device, as the name suggests, is a virtual fence that prevents communication between two nodes. It is used to separate the failed node from accessing shared resources. If there are two nodes that access shared resources at the same time, a collision occurs; this might corrupt the shared data, which is the data inside the VM.

Such fencing is done automatically based on the configuration defined, because we cannot identify a real failure or a temporary hang on a node. If a node is really down, then a fencing action is not needed, but if it is a temporary hang due to a network delay or temporary resource shortage, the suspected failure node will try to access a shared resource, which is harmful for our data. Now, let's see what happens if there is no fencing device:

- During normal operation, only the production node (**Proxmox SRV 1**) accesses the shared storage, while the configurations for the VMs are synchronized with a backup node. This is shown in the following diagram:

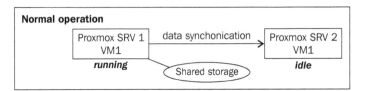

- If **Proxmox SRV1** is temporarily unreachable, **Proxmox SRV2** will start to replace it and access the shared storage, as shown in the following diagram:

- If **Proxmox SRV1** is recovered, it will access the shared storage to restore its service; this will lead to a collision. If both the VMs access the same file on a shared storage, the write operation from either one or both will fail. This is shown in the following diagram:

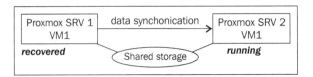

Available fencing device options

It is very important to protect our data from any corruption. What types of fencing devices are available and how can they build their fences during node failure? There are two fencing options that are listed in the following points:

- **Power fencing**: In this, both the nodes are added to the fencing device for monitoring. If there is any suspicious failure on the production node for a period of time, the fencing device simply turns off the power of the outlet to which the affected server is connected, while the backup node will take over the position of the failed node to provide the required services. For the failed node, the power switch will send a notification to the system administrator and a manual recovery is required, but no service interruption will occur on the client side. Here are some manufacturers that manufacture a monitored **power distribution unit (PDU)**:
    - APC: `http://www.apc.com/products/family/?id=136`
    - IBM: `http://www-03.ibm.com/systems/x/options/rackandpower/powerdistributionmonitored.html`

    The monitored PDU offers an administration panel that displays power consumptions on each outlet for monitoring, which allows us to turn off only the outlet connected to the failure node. Also, there is an e-mail notification function that should allow the system to send an e-mail alert to a system administrator if there is a power problem. The following diagram shows how it is actually done:

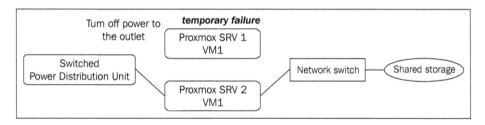

    When **Proxmox SRV1** encounters a temporary failure, PDU will detect this problem and turn off the power of **Proxmox SRV1**.

- **Network fencing**: In this, the server nodes are connected to a network switch instead of the power switch. There are two types of network fencing:

- **IPMI (Intelligent Platform Management Interface)**: This requires a separate **IMPI card** or *onboard IPMI port* to function. In a running operating system, periodic query checks can be performed to ensure the accessibility of the monitored server. If the query check fails many times, an IPMI message will be sent to this failed node to turn it off. The following diagram shows how it operates:

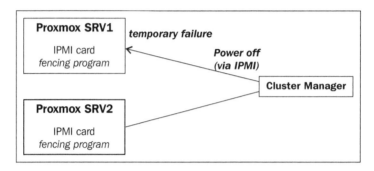

- **SNMP (Simple Network Management Protocol)**: When there is suspicious failure on a server node in a period of time, the network port between the network switch and the failed server is disabled; this prevents the failed server from accessing the shared storage. When the operator requires us to turn the server back on, manual configuration is required. Here is how it operates:

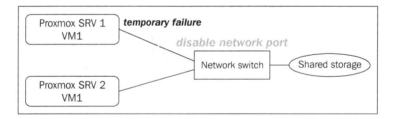

Hence, by separating the failed **Proxmox SRV1**, we can avoid multiple accesses to the shared storage and make room for us to fix the failure.

Intelligent Platform Management Interface (IPMI)

We mentioned IPMI earlier in the network fencing section; it is an important feature of network fencing. So, let's look at it in more detail.

IPMI is a standardized interface and a protocol that provides system-level management software for system administration. IPMI runs separately from an operating system, which means that it will not be affected during an operating system crash. It is not implemented in a normal motherboard, but it's only available on a server-level motherboard. IPMI functions can be used in the following three scenarios:

- During the boot-up process before starting the operating system
- When the system is powered down
- In the case of a system failure

In our infrastructure setting, we will make use of this remote power-off function to ensure data integrity. What if the network port connected to the affected server is cut? **Simple network management protocol (SNMP)** is used instead.

Simple network management protocol (SNMP)

Similar to the IMPI protocol, system administrators are able to manage devices over IP with SNMP. Unlike IPMI, many motherboards accept SNMP commands as it is a built-in function of the network interface card. The monitored devices are running SNMP agents, which transfer the management information to the SNMP server (also called manager). The SNMP agent can be processed in a *read-only* or *read-write* mode. The following diagram shows the structure of SNMP:

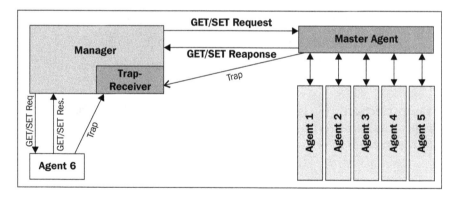

As shown in the preceding diagram, if the agent is running in the read-write mode, the *SNMP manager* is able to change the SNMP configuration at agent side with *SET request*. Another important part is the SNMP trap. The **SNMP trap** enables asynchronous notification between the agent and the manager by notifying significant events with unsolicited SNMP message. By examining the SNMP trap messages, the switch is able to disable the proper port to finish the fencing function.

Key component 4 – quorum disk

A quorum disk is a small shared storage in a cluster design, and it is necessary for a two-node Proxmox cluster to work properly. As we only have two member nodes in a cluster, it will cause racing problems when one of the nodes is down. In our example, we would like to use a disk-based quorum daemon — **qdisk** — to solve this problem. The functionalities of a qdisk are listed as follows:

- **Heartbeat and liveliness determination**: Node updates the status blocks on a quorum disk and alters the timestamp, which is used to decide whether a node has hung or not. If there are certain misses during the heuristics testing, a node is declared as offline.

- **Scoring and heuristics**: As mentioned in the previous point, up to 10 heuristics (minimum 1 heuristic) can be configured by the administrator. There is a score for each heuristic. Normally, there are multiple heuristics defined in a cluster configuration. A node is defined as healthy only if it has scored half of the total maximum score. If the score drops too low for a node, it will remove itself from the cluster by rebooting. An example of setting up heuristics is shown in the following command:

```
<heuristic interval="3" program="ping $GATEWAY -c1 -w1" score="1"
tko="4"/>
```

  This command contains of the following parts:

  - **Interval**: This is the time to wait between each test
  - **Program**: This is the heuristic testing to perform
  - **TKO**: This defines the number of "misses" before marking the node as dead

- **Master election**: This is an important process for a cluster, because there is only one node that can be elected as the *master*. The voting process is simple; a member node with a lower node ID wins. For more details, refer to *Chapter 4, Configuring a Proxmox VE Cluster*.

The process of qdisk can be summarized as follows:

- The cluster manager believes that the node is online.
- This node has made enough consecutive, timely writes to the quorum disk.
- The node has a high enough score to consider itself online. For more details on the structure of qdisk, refer to http://linux.die.net/man/5/qdisk.

Summary

In this chapter, we went through the key components that are needed for a HA Proxmox cluster. We used a stored storage to save data for a VM, a reliable dedicated/isolated network to allow data communication between the VM server, nodes, and storage. Also, we learned that we can use fencing devices as the data protection point if there are any failures. Different filesystems were introduced with explanations of their characteristics.

In the next chapter, we will demonstrate how to build a HA cluster with Proxmox with a practical configuration, and most of the concepts learned in this chapter will be used.

4
Configuring a Proxmox VE Cluster

So far, we have learned all the background knowledge required to work on a Proxmox VE cluster. I think you should be very excited to play with it on your own. In this chapter, we are going to cover the following topics:

- Configuring a network for a Proxmox VE cluster
- Preparing storage for a Proxmox cluster
- Configuring a Proxmox VE cluster
- Network fencing using a Cisco switch via SNMP
- Building a Gluster filesystem for a Proxmox cluster
- Building a Ceph filesystem for a Proxmox cluster

Configuring a network for a Proxmox VE cluster

We have mentioned that a network with redundancy is needed for a HA environment. As most of our services are based on networks, avoiding network failure is an important task for us. So how can we build that?

Building a network with redundancy

Since there is a lot of internal traffic including health check messages, data transferring from/to a shared storage, and SNMP messages, a high-speed network that *allows a gigabit Ethernet connection* is recommended.

For our testing environment, we used two Cisco Catalyst 2950 switches that have 24 Fast Ethernet ports each operating at 100 Mb/s. These switches are interconnected to ensure there is no single point of failure. Since multiple fencing methods will be demonstrated, an SNMP server will be configured for the network switches too.

Building a separate network for the Proxmox VE cluster

In *Chapter 1, Basic Concepts of a Proxmox Virtual Environment*, we successfully created our own VMs using the default settings. In my opinion, it will be better to use a separate network between the management network of Proxmox and VMs. It is much better if we can use a separate network for the VE as it will help us *reduce the chances of leaking user credentials*.

There are two methods to achieve this goal: IP subnetting and Virtual LAN tagging. Let's talk about the network options provided by Proxmox first.

Introducing Proxmox's network options

There are different network options available under Proxmox; the default option is a **bridged interface** and the other options supported by Proxmox are **routed interface**, **NAT**, and **bonding interface**, which are explained in more detail in the following list:

- The **bridged interface** allows the VMs to behave as if they are *directly connected to a physical network*.

- The **routed interface** makes the interface act like a *network router*. It responds to the **ARP (Address Resolution Protocol)** request packet from one network and uses the `proxy_arp` function to deliver a reply back to the network that the VMs need to reply to. The following diagram illustrates this in detail:

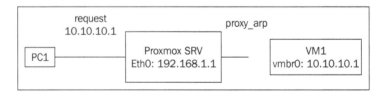

- The **NAT** interface normally applies to the physical interface that contains the Internet address. Such a configuration makes use of the **network address translation (NAT)** function provided by `iptables` by masquerading the traffic when it detects a packet that is coming from a specific network. It is similar to the routed interface but the NAT interface is more concentrated on Internet access. The following diagram illustrates this in detail:

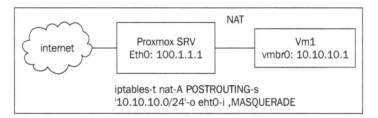

- There is a special network option for a Proxmox-named **bonding device**, which will be introduced in the *The concept on bonding device* section.

In the next section, we will delve deeper and learn the network concept of **virtual LAN (VLAN)** tagging, which is used to divide a network.

Introducing the VLAN structure

Modern networking can be further divided into seven layers of the **Open Systems Interconnection (OSI)** model. In a normal operation, we focus on layer 3 — the network layer, which allows IP addressing and routing.

Under the network layer, machines are able to communicate with their assigned IP addresses if they are within the same network, by calculating their subnet masks. Applying subnets on machines are actually reducing the number of machines in the same scope.

On the other hand, VLAN is enlarging the scope by grouping multiple switch ports in layer 2 — the data link layer. VLAN tagging is based on the standard under *IEEE 802.1Q*, which allows *up to 4,094 VLANs*.

Tagged VLAN makes use of the VLAN tagging technique where a *tagged packet* has a *VLAN ID* embedded in the tag while an untagged packet does not. To handle this kind of traffic, *access* and *trunk ports* are defined in the following points:

- **Access port**: This represents the port that contains the *untagged traffic*. If we do not configure the VLAN for an access port, the entire *untagged* traffic is delivered under the **default VLAN (VLAN1)**, which is also called **access VLAN**, while *dropping the traffic that was tagged*.

- **Trunk port**: This allows both *tagged* and *untagged* traffic with different VLANs running through. In this mode, packets are handled in different ways, which are explained as follows:

  ○ **For untagged packets**: If a native VLAN is configured, the switch will *tag the packets for native VLAN*. If not, it is tagged with the default VLAN. The packets will then be sent to all the ports with the same VLAN.

  ○ **For tagged packets**: If there is only one port assigned as a trunk port, all tagged packets are delivered to this port. When the packet reaches a trunk port, it is examined and delivered only if it is within the allowed VLAN. If the allowed VLAN is not configured, the VLAN's traffic is allowed by default. Then, the packet is sent to all the switch ports with the same configured VLAN.

Therefore, the *access VLAN* setting of the access port must match the *native VLAN* setting of the trunk port when we want the packets to be successfully delivered.

In the following example, we have two tagged packets with **VLAN10** and **VLAN20** being sent to the *trunk port*. In the trunk port, they are configured to have the *default settings*. We have two PCs, **PC1** and **PC2**, connected to two **access ports** configured with **VLAN10** and **VLAN20** respectively.

Since there is only one trunk port, all of the tagged traffic is sent to it. When both the tagged packets arrive in the trunk port at **Switch 1**, both the packets are allowed because the trunk port in a Cisco switch *allows all VLAN traffic by default*. This has been depicted in the following diagram:

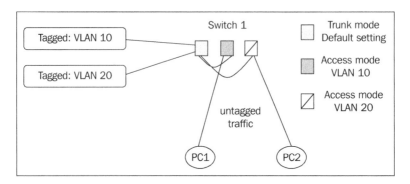

The following example is similar to the previous one, but this time, the switch *allows only VLAN10 traffic*. Assuming we have two tagged packets, one is tagged with **VLAN10** and the other one is tagged with **VLAN20**. When both these packets arrive in the trunk port at **Switch 1**, the packet with the **VLAN20** tag is dropped because only the **VLAN10** traffic is allowed. This is shown in the following diagram:

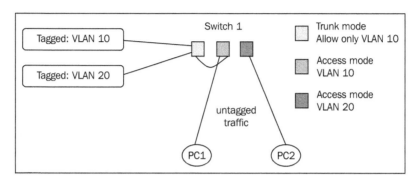

In the following example, when one untagged packet reaches the trunk port at **Switch 1**, the packet is tagged with the default VLAN1 tag, but there is no device connected with VLAN1. Therefore, the packet is dropped, as depicted in the following diagram:

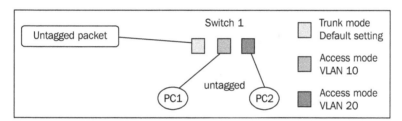

In the following example, we have a similar configuration as that of the previous example, with the exception that the trunk mode is configured with the native VLAN tag. The untagged packet will then be tagged with **VLAN10**, which is therefore able to reach **PC1**, as shown in the following diagram:

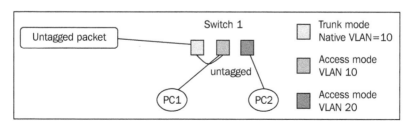

We have gone through some concepts about VLAN; now, let's check out how we can implement it under our VE.

Creating an infrastructure for a Proxmox cluster testing environment

Now, we have learned the concept of virtual network. Let's check the infrastructures we are going to build in this chapter. To start with, let's build our cluster with DRBD enabled, as shown in the following diagram:

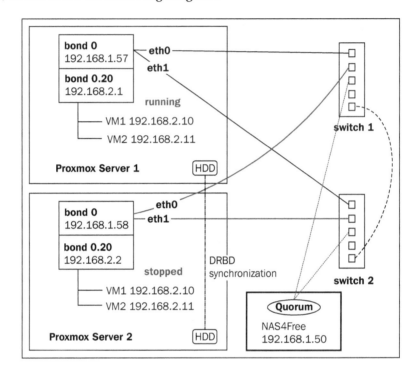

To achieve HA, *two network cards* and *two network switches* are used. Here, **VLAN20** is set up for the VMs for security purposes.

A cluster has to define which node is currently acting as the primary role. Therefore, a *voting system* is used to check whether the cluster is dead or primary node switching is needed. A small storage called **quorum** is used to help the cluster make this decision.

The concept of a quorum device

The voting system is a democratic system, which means that there is one *vote* for each node. So, if we only have two nodes, no one can win the race, which causes the *racing problem*. As a result, we need to add a third node joining this system (quorum, in our case). The following is a sample diagram on why the racing problem appears and how we can fix it:

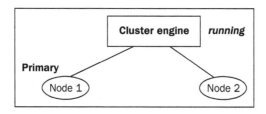

Assume that we have a cluster system with only two nodes; the preceding diagram shows the initial state of the cluster. We have marked **Node 1** as the **Primary** node. The following diagram shows the problem with this node:

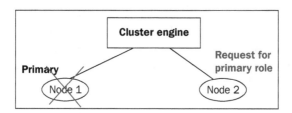

Here, **Node 1** is disconnected, and therefore **Node 2** will take over its position to become the primary node. However, it cannot be successful because two votes are needed for a role-switching operation to complete. Therefore, the cluster will become *non-operational* until **Node 1** is recovered, as shown in the following diagram:

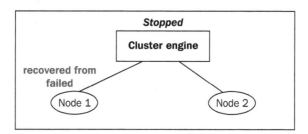

When **Node 1** has recovered from a failure, it tries to join back with the cluster but fails to do so because the cluster has stopped working.

To solve this problem, it is recommended to add an extra node to the cluster in order to create a HA environment. The following diagram shows an example of where a node failed and **Node 2** would like to be the primary node:

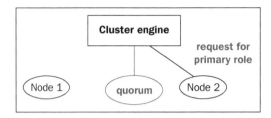

When there is a similar condition of a node going down, we have one more node to decide who will win the race. Therefore, the one missing node will not cause the cluster to stop.

The concept of a bonding device

For the network interface, a **bonding device** (**Bond0** and **Bond1**) will be created in the Proxmox VE. This bonding device is also called **NIC teaming**, which is a native Linux kernel feature that allows users to double the network speed performance or add network redundancy. There are two options for network redundancy, *802.1ad* and *Active-backup*. They have different response patterns when handling multiple sessions, shown in the following diagram:

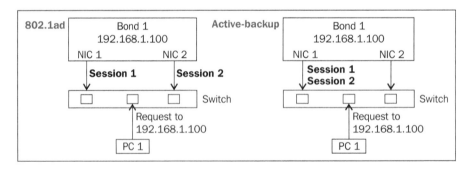

These network redundancy options are explained in the following points:

- In **802.1ad**, both the network interfaces are active; therefore, the sessions can be processed by a different network card, which is an *active-active* model.
- On the other hand, only *one* interface is in the active state in the **Active-backup** mode. The backup interface will become active only if one active session fails.

The concept of DRBD

Since we need to have identical data in both the Proxmox servers, using DRBD allows us to build a network-based RAID 1.

With this structure, we are able to perform online migration without putting our VMs down. If we perform a normal shutdown on one node, *all of the VMs will then be switched to another operating cluster node*. Therefore, *pay attention to maintaining the available system resources*. If the system resources are not enough to run all the VMs, then the services are likely to be stopped, as shown in the following diagram:

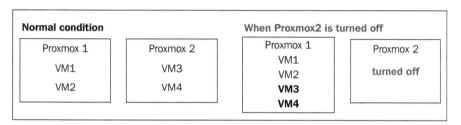

If we change the storage option from network RAID 1 to *Gluster filesystem*, the infrastructure will change, as shown in the following diagram:

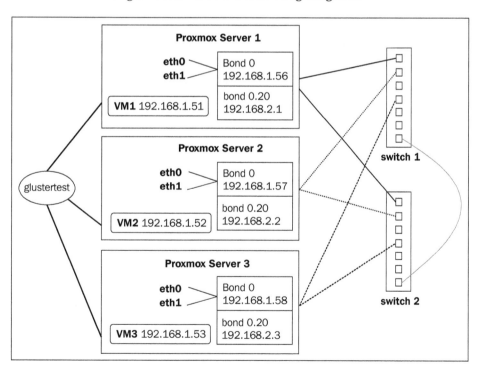

In this setting, we have configured shared storage with the Gluster filesystem inside three VMs. Of course, it would be much better if we have a unique storage cluster. A GlusterFS named `glustertest` is created with the following structure:

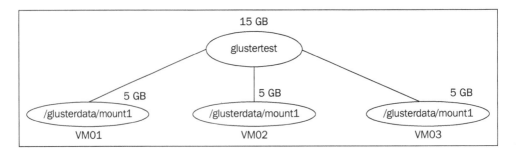

For each VM, I have created a directory to be shared at `/glusterdata` volume and a subdirectory, `mount1`, is created. In the Gluster concept, we have to create subdirectories under the root mount point. Such a subdirectory is called a **brick**. Therefore, a single mount point can be used to form multiple bricks for different volumes. Here is an example of multiple bricks with a single mount point:

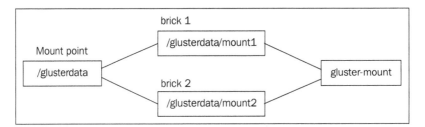

In this diagram, a single mount point, `/glusterdata`, is defined while `mount1` and `mount2` are shared with the volume as storage. Therefore, we can store our VMs under this distributed filesystem, which enhances the availability.

Also, we will check how to build the cluster with another distributed filesystem, Ceph, as depicted in the following diagram:

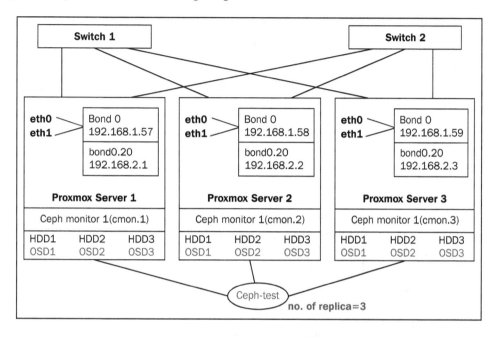

A three-node cluster is built because three monitors and one OSD is the minimal requirement for a Ceph environment under Proxmox. Two-node clusters for Ceph is not available because of the following reasons:

- To ensure data safety, there must be at least one backup copy for a file. So, the minimum replica size is 2. If we have a two-node cluster for Ceph, the operation stops if a failed node is found.

- To prevent the racing condition between two Ceph member nodes (this was covered in the *The concept of a quorum device* section).

For testing purposes, the Ceph monitors will be installed in each Proxmox server and new hard drives will be added on three servers for the purpose of using Ceph as OSD.

As we mentioned in *Chapter 3, Key Components for Building a Proxmox VE Cluster*, we can specify the number of replicas for each placement group and we can set up three replicas for each file. When the setup is complete, we will try to store the VM images into the OSD, and further testing will be done after a system failure.

In the next part, a demonstration of the system's preparation for cluster creation is shown. Now, we will cover how to configure bonding devices for our cluster network.

Preparing a network for a Proxmox cluster

In order to provide the HA environment, we will choose to create a bonding device with the **active-backup** option. The following are the steps to create our own device:

1. Install two network adapters for the system first, with properly configured drivers.

2. If everything goes well, we should have network interfaces called `eth0` and `eth1` displayed as follows:

```
root@vmsrv01:~# ifconfig | grep eth
eth0      Link encap:Ethernet  HWaddr 00:19:d1:0b:91:6e
eth1      Link encap:Ethernet  HWaddr 00:19:d1:0b:91:6e
```

3. Now, we need to combine `eth0` and `eth1` into a bonding device – **bond0**. First, we will click on **vmsrv01** under **DataCenter** in the panel on the left-hand side of the web management console. Now, we choose the **Network** tab in the panel on the right-hand side and click on **Create** and then choose **Bond**, which will initialize a create bond window. Enter the following information in that window:

   ◦ **Name**: bond0

   ◦ **Slaves**: eth0 eth1

   ◦ **Mode**: Choose the `active-backup` method

4. For the VLAN interface of the VM, we need to edit the `/etc/network/interfaces` file and add the following code lines under the `iface bond0` block:

```
auto bond0.20
iface bond0.20 inet manual
        vlan-raw-device bond0
```

5. Next, we need to change the default network interface from `eth0` to `bond0` in order to have the *active-backup* network feature. We can double-click on the `vmbr0` interface to edit its properties, as shown in the following screenshot:

The following table lists the information to be configured in each server:

Server name	Device name	IP	Net mask	Bridge ports
Proxmox1	vmbr0	192.168.1.57	255.255.255.0	bond0
Proxmox2	vmbr0	192.168.1.58	255.255.255.0	bond0
Proxmox3	vmbr0	192.168.1.59	255.255.255.0	bond0

6. We also have to create a virtual bridge (vmbr1), which is used by the VMs. Click on **Create** in the menu on the top-hand side and choose **Bridge**; then insert the information provided in the following table:

Server name	Device name	IP	Subnet mask	Bridge ports
Proxmox1	vmbr1	192.168.2.1	255.255.255.0	bond0.20
Proxmox2	vmbr1	192.168.2.2	255.255.255.0	bond0.20
Proxmox3	vmbr1	192.168.2.3	255.255.255.0	bond0.20

7. We need to configure the hostname and the host table for each Proxmox server. Edit /etc/hostname for the local hostname and /etc/hosts for hostnames of other nodes and enter the following information in it:

Server name	/etc/hostname	/etc/hosts
Proxmox1	vmsrv01	• 192.168.1.57 vmsrv01 pvelocalhost • 192.168.1.58 vmsrv02 pvelocalhost • 192.168.1.59 vmsrv03 pvelocalhost
Proxmox2	vmsrv02	• 192.168.1.57 vmsrv01 pvelocalhost • 192.168.1.58 vmsrv02 pvelocalhost • 192.168.1.59 vmsrv03 pvelocalhost
Proxmox3	vmsrv03	• 192.168.1.57 vmsrv01 pvelocalhost • 192.168.1.58 vmsrv02 pvelocalhost • 192.168.1.59 vmsrv03 pvelocalhost

 The pvelocalhost is set up on each Proxmox server separately; do *not* use this keyword in every line.

8. Reboot the server to apply the changes. To verify that the bridging device has started, use the following command:

```
Root# brctl show
bridge name     bridge id              interfaces
vmbr0           8000.0019d10b916e      bond0
vmbr1           8000.0019d10b916e      bond0.20
```

 To save space, I have removed the STP enabled column.

Now, we have configured the network devices for the Proxmox VE and our VMs. Next, we are going to prepare the file storage for the Proxmox VE.

Preparing storage for a Proxmox cluster

In this section, we need to use multiple storage devices for demonstration; please prepare the following before starting with this section. The machine requirement can be either in the *physical* or *virtual* form:

- One machine should be installed with NAS4free with one extra hard drive as quorum
- Three machines are needed to install Proxmox nodes for CEPH storage
- A separate hard drive should be installed in each Proxmox node for DRBD storage
- Three dedicated machines with one extra hard drive is needed to set up GlusterFS storage

Now, we are going to prepare the storage on the cluster environment. There are different approaches available on the market; we will create shared storage via iSCSI with the NAS4free server.

Preparing iSCSI shared storage with NAS4free for the quorum device

NAS4free is a type of software-based network storage software under the FreeBSD operation system. There are many sharing methods available, but we will focus on using the iSCSI because a mounted drive via iSCSI can be treated as a local hard disk by Proxmox, which is very useful if we would like to create a quorum disk or to form a network RAID device. Before we demonstrate the process of setting up the iSCSI, we have to explain how the iSCSI actually works.

Basic concepts of an iSCSI device

iSCSI is created based on the concept of **SCSI (Small Computer System Interface)**, but iSCSI is network-based instead of physically-attached hardware via SCSI.

In iSCSI, there are some important terms we have to learn; these are **iSCSI portal**, **target**, **initiator**, **extent**, and **LUN (logical unit number)**, which are explained in more detail in the following points:

- **iSCSI portal**: This provides an IP with a network port pair for a client to connect with. The format for the portal is `<iSCSI_device_IP>:<network_port>`. This communication runs under the TCP connection.

- **iSCSI target**: This is the storage device(s) that allows the client to use the device after connecting to it via the iSCSI portal. The user's login information might be required to access the storage. Normally, this target is shipped with several hard disks to provide large storage space. The iSCSI target server is able to restrict the initiation of communication from a certain network only.

- **iSCSI initiator**: The user can make use of the iSCSI initiator program with the iSCSI portal for **discovery** or **auto-discovery**. Discovery is the process of requesting a list of targets and it gets a list of available types of storage.

- **Extent**: This is the physical location where the iSCSI server provides storage, and it can be further categorized into **file extent** and **device extent**.

- **LUN**: LUN stands for **logical unit number**. In SCSI, it is used to identify which device is referring to it in one SCSI channel. Each extent is mapped to a single LUN for the client to use in iSCSI.

The following diagram shows you the structure of iSCSI and it might give you an idea of what is happening:

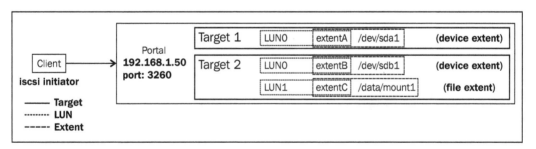

It's good for us to learn the basic concepts; now, it's time for us to practice what we have learned:

1. To be able to use newly-added hard disks in Nas4free, we need to import hard disks under **Disks | Management** and click on **Import disks** if you cannot find your hard drives. Then, we should see the internal hard disks as listed in the following screenshot:

Device	Device model	Size	Serial number	Controller	Controller model
ada0	QEMU HARDDISK	10240MB	QM00001	ata0	Intel PIIX3 WDMA2 controller
ada1	QEMU HARDDISK	10240MB	QM00005	ahcich0	Intel ICH9 AHCI SATA controller

Import disks	Clear config and Import disks	Rescan disks

If you installed NAS4free in a KVM-based VM under Proxmox and found that the attached hard disks could not be detected in NAS4free, you can try using the virtio bus and perform a system reboot.

2. Then, we have to set up the iSCSI-related information in **Services | iSCSI target**. The following window will appear and we have to tick the **Enable** option in the right corner. Next, we have to define the base name for iSCSI targeting. This value begins with `iqn` (for more information, please refer to *Chapter 3, Key Components for Building a Proxmox VE Cluster*). Accept the default settings and click on **Save and Restart** at the bottom to start the service:

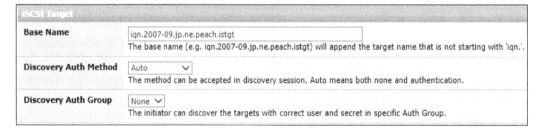

iSCSI Target	
Base Name	iqn.2007-09.jp.ne.peach.istgt
	The base name (e.g. iqn.2007-09.jp.ne.peach.istgt) will append the target name that is not starting with 'iqn.'.
Discovery Auth Method	Auto ∨
	The method can be accepted in discovery session. Auto means both none and authentication.
Discovery Auth Group	None ∨
	The initiator can discover the targets with correct user and secret in specific Auth Group.

3. Next, an extent should be defined, which is either file-based or device-based. In the following screenshot, we have defined device-based sharing:

If you wish to create a *file-based* device, you can do so with the help of the following steps:

1. In the top menu, click on **Advanced** and choose **Command**, as shown in the following screenshot:

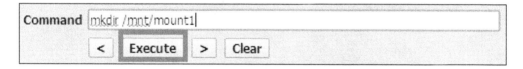

2. Create a new folder under /mnt, and name it mount1, as shown in the following screenshot:

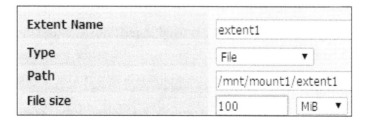

3. If no error is found, we can add a file extent, as shown in the following screenshot:

Extent Name	extent1
Type	File ▼
Path	/mnt/mount1/extent1
File size	100	MiB ▼

Here, we will store the new data in a new file called extent1. After changing the settings, remember to click on **Apply changes**.

4. After that, we have to configure the *initiator*; we will see a window similar to the following:

Tag number	1
Initiators	ALL
Authorised network	192.168.1.0/24

5. Then, we have to set up a *portal* for the client connection; press the plus (**+**) button and enter the information in the `<IP_address>:<port_num>` format, for example `192.168.1.50:3260`, as shown in the following screenshot:

Tag number	1
Portals	192.168.1.50:3260

6. Finally, we can configure the iSCSI target, which is the target disk that we allow the user to use, as shown in the following screenshot:

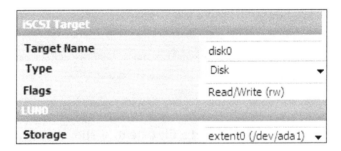

Here are the settings that appear in this window:

- **Target Name**: This field is used to indicate a shared device
- **Type**: This field is used to choose a *disk* as the local storage
- **Flags**: This field is used to set the **read/write (rw)** permission in order to allow writing to a disk
- **LUN0**: We need to use this field only to share single storage

At this point, we have configured a file storage that allows us to connect via the iSCSI protocol. In the next section, we will proceed with building our own cluster.

Configuring a Proxmox VE cluster

Now, we are going to the core part of what this book covers, that is, building a cluster with HA. Do you have everything you need now? Here is a list for you to go over quickly:

The following is the hardware checklist:

- Two servers installed with the Proxmox server.
- Shared storage that is accessible to all servers as quorum and VM storage. Such storage can be built using NAS4free or other alternatives; here, I have configured a NAS4free server with the IP address as 192.168.1.50.
- Two network cards on each server connected separately to the two network switches to test the network-fencing ability.

The following is the software checklist:

- Proxmox servers are configured with the network settings mentioned before and should be able to ping each other
- Bonding devices **Bond0** and **Bond1** should be well configured

To minimize the number of physical machines needed, I will demonstrate building up a two-node cluster for you. However, please note that the *two-node cluster should be used in the testing platform only*; a true cluster is built with at least three nodes.

Forming a two-node cluster with DRBD

We have to build our cluster under the terminal, so make sure you can access the server with the root account. First, we choose Proxmox server 1 (vmsrv01) as the master and create a cluster called mycluster. Here are the steps:

1. Log in to vmsrv01, enter the following command, and wait for the output:

   Root# pvecm create mycluster

2. In Proxmox server 2 (vmsrv02), type in the following command:

   Root# pvecm add vmsrv01

3. You will get an output stating that the authenticity of the host vmsrv01 can't be established and it will ask if you want to continue; simply type yes to accept the connection. If everything goes fine, you will have an output that is similar to the one you got when you created the cluster earlier:

   ```
   Successfully added node 'vmsrv02' to cluster
   ```

4. If you already have the VMs running on the secondary nodes, you will fail to join the node to the cluster and you'll get the following message:

   ```
   This host already contains virtual machines - please remove
   the first
   ```

5. To solve this problem, you can move all of your VMs to your cluster's master node, for example `vmsrv01` in our case. The master node is able to create a new cluster even if you have VM(s) running on top of it.

6. After you have created a cluster and added two nodes to it, you will be able to control both servers via a web console on a single page, as shown in the following screenshot:

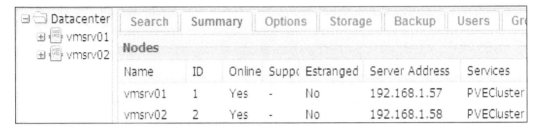

7. Next, we have to add a quorum to prevent a single point of failure. The iSCSI device is shared over the NAS4free server and is added to our system, as shown in the following screenshot:

8. The **Add: iSCSI** window is shown; here, we have to fill in the following information:

   ○ **ID**: This can contain any name that starts with a letter

   ○ **Portal**: We have already defined it; it is `192.168.1.50:3260`

- ○ **Use LUNs directly**: This should be unchecked, as shown in the following screenshot:

- ○ **Target**: You can simply press the ⌄ button to initialize *auto discovery*, as shown in the following screenshot:

9. At this point, we can accept the discovered value and we should have the new storage, as listed in the following screenshot:

10. Our new storage will also appear in the disk storage of each Proxmox server, as shown in the following screenshot:

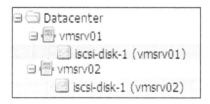

11. The detailed information will be shown when we click on the **Content** tab in the panel on the right-hand side:

Summary	Content	Permissions
Name	Format	Size ▲
⊟ Images (1 Item)		
CH 00 ID 0 LUN 0	raw	10.00GB

12. Here, we can see that **LUN0** comes with the iSCSI configuration. If we have configured multiple LUNs under NAS4free, it will be shown here accordingly, as shown in the following screenshot:

⊟ Images (2 Items)		
CH 00 ID 0 LUN 0	raw	10.00GB
CH 00 ID 0 LUN 1	raw	10.00GB

13. Then, we have to install the `iscsiadm` command on both Proxmox server to keep it connected to our iSCSI device on every boot. To enable this command, simply type the following in the command line:

```
Root# aptitude install tgt
```

14. Edit the `/etc/iscsi/iscsid_conf` file, change `node.startup` from `manual` to `automatic` as follows:

```
node.startup="automatic"
```

15. Next, we need to make this new disk our quorum disk. Under CLI of `vmsrv01`, make sure you have a new disk and find it by using the following command:

```
Root# fdisk -l
Disk /dev/sdb: 10.7 GB, 10737418240 bytes
```

16. Assuming that there is a new disk in `/dev/sdb` on `vmsrv01`, we can create the quorum disk by using the following command:

```
root@vmsrv01# mkqdisk -c /dev/sdb -l proxmox_quorum1
```

17. In the previous code, `/dev/sdb` is the iSCSI device we have mounted, and `proxmox_quorum1` is the quorum disk identifier that will be used later. When prompted about destroying all data, type `y` to accept the operation as shown in the following command:

```
Writing new quorum disk label 'proxmox_quorum1' to /dev/sdb
WARNING: About to destroy all data on /dev/sdb; proceed [N/y]? y
```

18. We must include the quorum in the cluster configuration file to make it work. To update the cluster configuration, we have a special procedure as recommended by Proxmox. First, we need to copy the `cluster.conf` file to the `cluster.conf.new` file using the following command:

```
Root# cp /etc/pve/cluster.conf /etc/pve/cluster.conf.new
```

19. Next, we need to update `/etc/pve/cluster.conf.new` in different fields:

```
<cluster name="mycluster" config_version="2">
```

This code should be updated to the following:

```
<cluster name="mycluster" config_version="3">
```

 The value of `config_version` should be increased by 1 for every new modification.

20. The preceding code simply tells the system that our cluster configuration file has changed. The `cman` parameters should also be updated as follows:

```
<cman keyfile="/var/lib/pve-cluster/corosync.authkey"></cman>
```

This code should be updated to the following:

```
<cman keyfile="/var/lib/pve-cluster/corosync.authkey"
expected_votes="3"></cman>
```

21. The preceding code tells the system that the `expected_votes` is 3 because we now have three nodes after adding the quorum disk as one node to avoid cluster failure if one node fails. Add the following code after the `</cman>` tag to include the quorum disk:

```
<quorumd votes="1" allow_kill="0" interval="1" label="proxmox_
quorum1" tko="10">
   <heuristic interval="3" program="ping $GATEWAY -c1 -w1"
     score="1" tko="4"/>
   <heuristic interval="3" program="ip addr | grep bond0 | grep
     -q UP" score="2" tko="3"/>
</quorumd>
<totem token="30000" />
```

Here we have defined:

- The quorum disk with label as "**proxmox_quorum1**"
- The waiting time for a heartbeat message as 30 seconds
- Heuristic checks on a network node is required by the quorum disk

If we simply edit the `cluster.conf` file without making a backup copy, it might not be replicated to other nodes via corosync. If this happens, the configuration of a cluster is not synchronized, and it will likely lead to cluster failure! Therefore, follow the instructions provided.

22. Get back to the web management console, click on the **Datacenter** folder on the left panel, and choose **HA** from the top menu of the panel on the right-hand side, as shown in the following screenshot:

23. We can see that there is a pending change in the following window:

```
Pending changes
--- /etc/pve/cluster.conf        2014-04-19 00:10:59.000000000 +0800
+++ /etc/pve/cluster.conf.new    2014-04-19 16:46:02.000000000 +0800
```

The change will only be detected if we create a `.new` file; if we change the `cluster.conf` file directly, changes will not be detected.

24. We can click on **Activate** and **confirm** to make changes. Now, we have to reload the cluster configuration files with the following command:

```
Root# /etc/init.d/cman reload
```

So far, we have configured a cluster that allows us to have one failure node. In this setting, live migration and HA are not available yet because shared storage for VMs has not been defined. Therefore, we need to install the DRBD packages to form our network RAID device for our VMs.

Installing and configuring DRBD

According to the information provided on the DRBD homepage, DRBD packages have been shipped into Linux kernel versions above the 2.6.32 release. Unfortunately, Proxmox comes with Linux kernel Version 2.6.32; you can look at it yourself in the command line with the following command:

```
Root# uname -a
```

This should give you the following output:

```
Linux vmsrv02 2.6.32-28-pve #1 SMP x86_64 GNU/Linux
```

I have highlighted the kernel version and you should see that Proxmox is running on the 2.6.32 Linux kernel. So, we have to install DRBD packages manually on both servers. To simplify the installation process, I will install the package with the `apt-get` command. Here are the steps:

1. First, we have to log in to the terminal of vmsrv01 and issue the following command:

   root@vmsrv01# apt-get install drbd8-utils

2. When the installation has finished, load the DRBD kernel module by using the following command:

   root@vmsrv01# modprobe drbd

3. To check whether DRBD is running, use the following command:

   root@vmsrv01# lsmod | grep drbd

4. You should get output that is similar to the following one:

   drbd   339667   0

5. Ensure that you have installed DRBD packages in both cluster nodes. The next step is to create a configuration file under the `/etc/drbd.d/` directory. We need to create a new configuration file named `proxmox_drdb.conf` in `/etc/drbd.d/` on both the nodes. Let's check which options we have to set up first:

   In the **global** section, we have to change the value of **usage-count** from **yes** to **no**. The **usage-count** is used by `www.DRBD.org` to collect the number of installations, and it is not necessary to enable it. In the **common** section, we have to configure how DRBD handles write I/O:

   ○ **Protocol**: The available options for this are A, B, or C. Here, we are using *Protocol C*

      ○ Protocol A: In this, the write I/O is reported as completed if it has reached the local disk and the local TCP send buffer

      ○ Protocol B: In this, the write I/O is reported as completed if it has reached the local disk and the remote buffer cache

      ○ Protocol C: In this, the write IO is reported as completed if it has reached both the local and remote disk

   In the **startup** section, we can configure the timeout settings:

      ○ `wfc-timeout`: This is used when the cluster is starting up, and indicates how much time to wait for the connection from another node. The default value is unlimited, and we set it to `120 seconds` *to prevent unlimited waiting*.

- `degr-wfc-timeout`: This is used when the cluster is degraded (with one node left), and indicates how much time to wait for the connection. The default value for this is unlimited, and we set it to `60 seconds`.

- `become-primary-on`: Its value can be the *hostname* or `both`. If it is not set, both nodes are secondary nodes. Since both nodes are required to write data, we set the value to `both`.

In the **net** section, we have to configure the security setting and handles for split brain:

- `cram-hmac-alg`: With this, we can define which HMAC algorithm to use during the peer handshake connection. We use the `SHA1` algorithm.

- `shared-secret`: This is used with the `cram-hmac-alg` option to share the secret password for encryption.

- `allow-two-primaries`: We should enable this option because we have configured both the nodes to be in the primary node.

- `after-sb-0pri`: This is used after split-brain when no primary node is found. Therefore, it is used to synchronize data that has changed on the disk. We use the `discard-zero-changes` option with it.

- `after-sb-1pri`: This is used after split-brain when one primary node is left. We will discard any changes from the secondary node using the `discard-secondary` option.

- `after-sb-2pris`: This is used after split-brain, when both nodes claim to be the primary node. It is better to *disconnect* both nodes to prevent data corruption.

In the **syncer** section, we need to configure the synchronizer's behavior:

- `rate`: This is used to set the bandwidth (calculated in *bytes*). Please use around 30 to 50 percent of your total bandwidth. For example, I will use *100/8 * 0.3 ~ 4 M*.

  For *gigabit* Ethernet, the suggested value is between *40 M and 62.5 M*.

- `verify-alg`: This is used to verify the data content with the help of the MD5 algorithm.

After combining all these options, we get the following code:

```
global {
    usage-count no;
}
common {
    protocol C;
    startup {
        wfc-timeout 120;
        degr-wfc-timeout 60;
        become-primary-on both;
    }
    net {
        cram-hmac-alg sha1;
        shared-secret "password";
        allow-two-primaries;
        after-sb-0pri discard-zero-changes;
        after-sb-1pri discard-secondary;
        after-sb-2pri disconnect;
    }
    syncer {
        rate        4M;
        verify-alg  md5;
    }
}
```

In the next part, we will set up the disk configurations for DRBD. Also, we have to set up our hard disks with the `fdisk` command; for example, if we have a hard disk in `/dev/sdX`, we need to make a partition on it by using the following command:

```
Root# fdisk /dev/sdX
```

Here, X refers to the drive letter system assigned; I have `/dev/sdc` now. Just accept the default setting and you should have a device called `/dev/sdc1`.

6. We have to create the `r1.res` file under `/etc/drbd.d/` on both the nodes. Assume that we have the following disk drive with the same capacity:

Servers	Disk drive
vmsrv01, vmsrv02	/dev/sdc1

The final code will look as follows:

```
resource r1 {
    on vmsrv01 {
        device /dev/drbd1;
        disk   /dev/sdc1;
        address 192.168.1.57:7788;
        meta-disk internal;
    }
    on vmsrv02 {
        device /dev/drbd1;
        disk   /dev/sdc1;
        address 192.168.1.58:7788;
        meta-disk internal;
    }
}
```

> The default connection port is 7788 and we use the *local disk for metadata.*

7. Now, we have to include the files in the /etc/drbd.conf file, as shown in the following code snippet:

```
#include "drbd.d/global_common.conf"
include "drbd.d/proxmox_drbd.conf"
```

Here, the r1.res resource file is already included because there is a rule:

```
include "drbd.d/*.res"
```

8. Now, we can start the *DRBD service on both nodes* using the following command:

```
Root# /etc/init.d/drbd start
```

9. After that, we should be able to see output similar to the following output:

```
1: State change failed: (-2) Need access to UpToDate data
```

10. If we check the status of the DRBD service, it shows that it is not configured, as shown in the following command:

```
root@vmsrv01# service drbd status

drbd driver loaded OK; device status:

1:r1    Unconfigured
```

11. This means that we have to create the metadata now. We have to issue the following command:

```
Root# drbdadm create-md r1
```

12. Now, when we check the status, it will have a different output:

```
m:res cs          ro                      ds                       p mounted fstype
1:r1  Connected Secondary/Secondary   Inconsistent/Inconsistent   C
```

13. Currently, both the nodes are treating themselves as secondary nodes because they don't know whether they have the up-to-date data. To fix this problem, we need to make the following change in vmsrv01:

```
Root@vmsrv01# drbdadm -- --overwrite-data-of-peer \
primary r1
```

14. If this command executes successfully, when we check the status of DRBD on vmsrv01, you will see that it says it is up to date. In the following screenshot, vmsrv01 is trying to synchronize its data to vmsrv02 and it is processed till **0.9%**. The synchronization process usually takes a long time.

```
m:res    cs          ro         ds                  p mounted fstype
...      sync'ed:    0.9%       (10148/10236)M
1:r1     SyncSource  Primary/Secondary UpToDate/Inconsistent C
```

15. When finished, we can see that the status of vmsrv02 has changed to **UpToDate** but it is still in a **Secondary** role, as shown in the following screenshot:

```
m:res cs          ro                    ds                p mounted fstype
1:r1  Connected Primary/Secondary UpToDate/UpToDate C
```

16. To make vmsrv02 primary, we have to restart the DRBD service in the terminal of vmsrv02:

```
root@Vmsrv02# /etc/init.d/drbd restart
```

17. Now, vmsrv02 has changed to the primary role, as shown in the following screenshot:

```
m:res    cs          ro                ds                p mounted fstype
1:r1     Connected   Primary/Primary UpToDate/UpToDate   C
```

So far, we have created a DRBD volume but we have to build a filesystem on top of it for Proxmox to use. We are going to build it into a LVM volume.

Creating an LVM volume based on the DRBD shared storage

First, we have to enable a clustered LVM by editing the `/etc/lvm/lvm.conf` file on *both* the nodes and make the following change:

```
locking_type = 3
```

By default, the LVM locking type is set to 0, which is used for local file-based locking. We are changing it to 3 because we would like to have *cluster-level locking*, which prevents simultaneous access to the LVM volume.

Next, we need to enable the clustered LVM service by editing `/etc/init.d/clvm` on *both* the nodes:

```
START_CLVM=yes
```

Activate the cluster LVM service with the following command:

```
root# /etc/init.d/clvm start
```

Now, we only need to create the LVM volume under a single node. Let's start the setup at `vmsrv01`:

1. Under `vmsrv01`, create a **physical volume** (**PV**) for the LVM using the following command:

    ```
    root@vmsrv01# pvcreate /dev/drbd1
    ```

     The `/dev/drbd1` volume is defined in the `r1.res` resource file.

2. You should be able to see `/dev/drbd1` become a PV after using the following commands:

    ```
    root@vmsrv01# pvscan

    PV          VG       Fmt  Attr PSize   PFree
    DRBDVol     drbd-vg  lvm2 a--  20.00g  12.00g
    ```

3. Then, we have to build a **Volume Group** (**VG**) using the following command:

    ```
    root@vmsrv01# vgcreate drbd-vg DRBDVol
    ```

4. You can these settings with the help of the following command:

```
Root@vmsrv01# vgs

VG        #PV #LV #SN Attr    VSize    VFree
drbd-vg    1   1    0 wz--nc 20.00g   12.00g
```

 In the attributes of the VG we created, make sure that the character c is present, indicating that it is a clustered LVM volume.

5. Add the LVM volume via the Proxmox GUI under **Datacenter | Storage**. Then, choose **Add | LVM** as shown in the following screenshot:

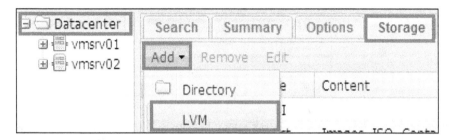

6. Follow the settings given in the following screenshot and make sure to check the **Shared** option:

7. We can only store KVM images in this LVM volume.

8. Create a KVM-based VM and install your preferred operating system with the following information:

Server ID	VM ID	VM name	VM type	IP	Storage
vmsrv02	201	drbd-kvm	KVM	192.168.2.11	drbd-vg, 4GB

9. Make sure you have chosen the `drbd-vg` LVM volume as the system storage, as shown in the following screenshot:

10. Start the VM and check the information of our storage:

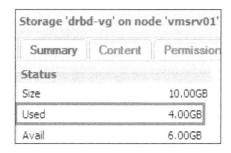

As you can see, we have allocated disk space for our KVM machine on the DRBD storage. Besides, we can also place an OpenVZ container with the DRBD storage, but we need to create a filesystem first. In this example, we will make use of the EXT4 filesystem as a demonstration; make sure you have made the following configurations in *both* nodes:

1. Create an LV in the DRBD volume group (`drbd-vg`) using the following command:

   ```
   root@vmsrv01# lvcreate -N drbd-ext4 -L 6G drbd-vg
   ```

2. Format the LV with the EXT4 filesystem using the following command:

   ```
   root@vmsrv01# mkfs.ext4 /dev/drbd-vg/drbd-ext4
   ```

3. Create a directory and mount the filesystem under it using the following command:

   ```
   root@vmsrv01# mkdir /drbd-store/ext4
   ```

   ```
   root@vmsrv01# mount /dev/drbd-vg/drbd-ext4 /drbd-store/ext4
   ```

4. We are able to use it for the OpenVZ container and add it as the directory storage. Unlike the storage for KVM, which is a clustered LVM storage, we are making our custom mount point for the OpenVZ containers, so we must *not* check the **Shared** option, as shown in the following screenshot:

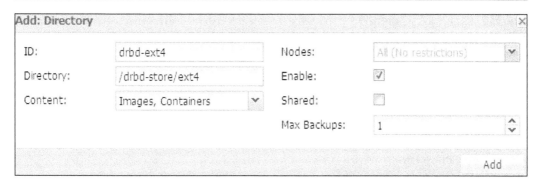

After that, we are able to place both the KVM and OpenVZ container under this storage, as shown in the following screenshot:

5. Then, create an OpenVZ container with the following information:

Server ID	VM ID	VM name	VM type	IP	Storage
vmsrv01	202	drbd-vz	openVZ	192.168.2.12	drbd-ext4, 4GB

Network fencing with a Cisco switch via SNMP

As we have mentioned before, we cannot enable the HA function if we don't have fencing devices on our cluster. When we check the HA service status, it gives an empty result, which means that the HA function is not enabled:

The HA-enabled VM creation process will be introduced in the next chapter. Let's take a look at what will happen if we try to enable HA on a VM at this point:

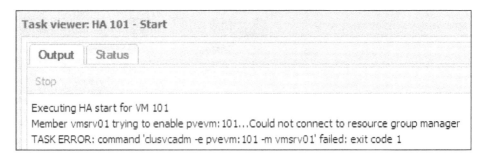

This error message simply tells us that when we try to enable HA on a VM, the HA service is not available, which causes error. The main reason for this is leaking fencing devices. In the next section, we are going to configure a fencing device with our Cisco switches. To make it easier, I will introduce the graphical tools for you to perform this task. If you are using a Linux platform as your workstation, you can simply execute the `screen` command, shown as follows:

root@workstation# screen /dev/ttyS0 9600

Assuming that we are using the Windows environment, we make use of a program called **HyperTerminal** to set up the IP addresses for the switches. For a Linux platform, we can use **minicom**.

> For the operation of minicom, please refer to http://www.
> cyberciti.biz/tips/connect-soekris-single-
> board-computer-using-minicom.html.

Configure the switches using the following steps:

1. First, you need to find out whether your serial port is mapped with the COM port. Do this by checking in the **Computer Management** window as shown in the following screenshot:

2. So, I have a **COM3** serial device and I have to set up the serial connection under HyperTerminal, as shown in the following screenshot:

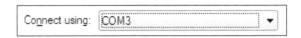

3. Then, we have to configure the following settings for the connection to work:

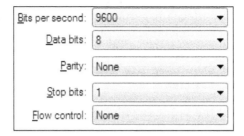

4. We can now configure the switch; please note that the *IP address for the switch will change* if you abide by the following instruction. *Do not* apply the switch configuration if you already have the IP settings applied! We issue the following commands in the switch:

```
Switch1> enable
Switch1# config terminal
Switch1(config)# interface vlan 1
Switch1(config-if)# ip address 192.168.1.45 255.255.255.0
Switch1(config-if)# no shut
```

5. We also need to check whether multicast traffic is allowed by your switches. Install the omping package on both the nodes with the following command:

```
root@vmsrv01# apt-get install omping
```

Issue the following command:

```
root@vmsrv01# omping vmsrv01 vmsrv02
```

If the multicast packets can be passed to another node, you should have an output similar to the following output:

```
vmsrv01 : multicast, seq=245, size=69 bytes, dist=0, time=0.468ms
```

6. After we have applied the IP address on **Switch 1**, we can apply another IP address, say `192.168.1.46`, to **Switch 2**. Our existing network infrastructure is similar to the structure shown in the following diagram:

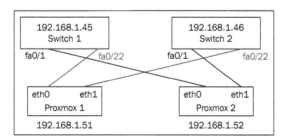

7. It's time for us to set up the SNMP service and define the network ports on the switch for network fencing. Before we can start our configuration, we have to check the interface properties, such as the index number (`ifIndex`) and description (`ifDescr`). For example, if we want to check the interface at `fa0/1`, issue the following command:

```
Switch1(config)# show snmp mib ifmib ifindex fa0/1
FastEthernet0/1: Ifindex = 1
```

Then we know that the `Ifindex` value equals to 1.

8. If you are unlucky like me and you've failed to execute the mentioned command, you have to enable the SNMP server on your switch to further check the interfaces; enter the following command to do so:

```
Switch1(config)# snmp-server community public ro
```

9. When the SNMP server is activated, we make use of the `snmpwalk` command to make the SNMP request switch; for example, we make the following request to Switch 2:

```
root@vmsrv01# snmpwalk -v 2c -c public 192.168.1.46
```

10. If we receive a huge amount of returning results, then your SNMP server on Switch 2 is active. Next, let's check the status of the Ethernet interfaces; the interface can be identified from the following pattern:

```
iso.3.6.1.2.1.2.2.1.<property_name>.<interface_name>
```

11. When we make our request, the `iso` keyword is replaced by `.1` as shown in the following snippet:

```
root@vmsrv01# snmpwalk -v 2c -c public 192.168.1.46 \
.1.3.6.1.2.1.2.2.1.2
```

12. The response shows the value of the `ifDescr` interface description:

```
iso.3.6.1.2.1.2.2.1.2.1 = STRING: "FastEthernet0/1".
```

13. This means we have successfully found the Ethernet port via SNMP; to check the interface index (`ifIndex`), use the following command:

```
root@vmsrv01# snmpwalk -v 2c -c public 192.168.1.46 \
.1.3.6.1.2.1.2.2.1.1
```

14. The values of `ifIndex` should return the following:

```
iso.3.6.1.2.1.2.2.1.1.1 = INTEGER: 1
```

15. Then, the values of `ifAdminStatus` should be `iso.3.6.1.2.1.2.2.1.1.7`:

```
iso.3.6.1.2.1.2.2.1.7.1 = INTEGER: 1.
```

16. Now, we can go back to the switch for configuration; remember to apply the commands *on both the switches*:

```
Switch1(config)# no snmp-server
Switch1(config)# interface fa0/1
Switch1(config-if)# description NODE2
Switch1(config-if)# interface fa0/22
Switch1(config-if)# description NODE1
```

17. Here, we have turned off the SNMP server if there is an existing one. Then, we named our interfaces NODE1 and NODE2. After that, an access list is created to restrict the SNMP server to be accessed by the Proxmox servers only for security reasons:

```
Switch1(config)# ip access-list standard MyclusterACL
Switch1(config-std-nacl)# permit 192.168.1.57
Switch1(config-std-nacl)# permit 192.168.1.58
Switch1(config-std-nacl)# deny any
```

18. It's now ready for us to create our own SNMP server for use. Unless further mentioned, the commands are executed under the configure terminal (configuration) mode:

```
snmp-server view Mycluster_view ifEntry.2.1 included
snmp-server view Mycluster_view ifEntry.2.22 included
snmp-server view Mycluster_view ifEntry.7.1 included
snmp-server view Mycluster_view ifEntry.7.22 included
snmp-server community Mycluster_community view Mycluster_view rw 1
Switch1(config)# exit
Switch1# write memory
```

19. In the Cisco switch command interface, ifEntry *is used to represent the string* – iso.3.6.1.2.1.2.2.1, and .2.1 is used to query *interface description* (ifDescr) for interface 1. Here is a list of objects we used in ifEntry:

    ○ 2 - ifDescr: This is used for the interface description, for example FastEthernet0/1

    ○ 7 - ifAdminStatus: This is used by the administrator to control the port status

20. We also have rw 1 at the end. The word rw means that it grants read-write permissions, and *number* 1 means that the access-list number 1 is used for access control.

We can check whether the SNMP server is working as expected, using the
`snmpwalk` command:

```
root@vmsrv01# snmpwalk -v 2c -c Mycluster_community 192.168.1.46

iso.3.6.1.2.1.2.2.1.2.1 = STRING:
FastEthernet0/1"iso.3.6.1.2.1.2.2.1.2.22 = STRING:
FastEthernet0/22"
iso.3.6.1.2.1.2.2.1.7.1 = INTEGER: 1
iso.3.6.1.2.1.2.2.1.7.22 = INTEGER: 1
```

21. Next, we have to restart the `cman` and `pve-cluster` service *on both the nodes*
    to apply the new settings:

    ```
    root@vmsrv01# /etc/init.d/cman restart
    ```

    ```
    root@vmsrv01# /etc/init.d/pve-cluster restart
    ```

22. After this, we will be able to test whether the fencing is working as expected
    with the following command:

    ```
    root@vmsrv01# fence_node vmsrv02 -vv
    ```

    If the command finished without any error, *all network interfaces for* `vmsrv02`
    will be turned off.

23. To enable a normal operation, we need to access *both the switches* and issue
    the following command:

    ```
    Switch1(config)# interface fa0/22
    ```

    ```
    Switch1(config-if)# no shut
    ```

24. After setting up the fencing devices on both the cluster nodes, some
    modifications must be made to the cluster's configuration file `/etc/pve/`
    `cluster.conf`. Remember to issue the following command before editing.
    Do not edit the file directly!

    ```
    root@vmsrv01# cp /etc/pve/cluster.conf  /etc/pve/cluster.conf.new
    ```

25. Edit the `/etc/pve/cluster/conf.new` file and add the records for *fencing*
    devices after the `<totem>` *tag*:

    ```
    <fencedevices>
        <fencedevice agent="fence_ifmib" community="Mycluster_
            community" ipaddr="192.168.1.45" name="fence_ifmib_SW1"
            snmp_version="2c" />
        <fencedevice agent="fence_ifmib" community="Mycluster_
            community" ipaddr="192.168.1.46" name="fence_ifmib_SW2"
            snmp_version="2c" />
    </fencedevices>
    ```

26. For the cluster node, we have to change the configuration file with the following pattern:

```
####################### From ##########################
<clusternode name="vmsrv01" nodeid="1" votes="1"/>
<clusternode name="vmsrv02" nodeid="2" votes="1"/>
#####################################################
####################### To ##########################
<clusternode name="NODE1" nodeid="1" votes="1">
  <fence>
    <method name="1">
      <device action="off" name="fence_ifmib_SW1"
        port="FastEthernet0/22"/>
      <device action="off" name="fence_ifmib_SW2"
        port="FastEthernet0/22"/>
    </method>
  </fence>
<unfence>
    <device action=on name=fence_ifmib_SW1 port=FastEthernet0/22/>
    <device action=on name=fence_ifmib_SW2 port=FastEthernet0/22/>
</unfence>
</clusternode>
<clusternode name="NODE2" nodeid="2" votes="1">
  <fence>
    <method name="1">
      <device action="off" name="fence_ifmib_SW1"
        port="FastEthernet0/1"/>
      <device action="off" name="fence_ifmib_SW2"
        port="FastEthernet0/1"/>
    </method>
  </fence>
<unfence>
    <device action=on name=fence_ifmib_SW1 port=FastEthernet0/1/>
    <device action=on name=fence_ifmib_SW2 port=FastEthernet0/1/>
</unfence>
</clusternode>
```

Make sure the `name` property under the `clusternode` tag matches the one that we previously defined inside our switches, and is listed under `/etc/hosts`. If not, the following error will be shown in `/var/log/messages`:

```
fence_ifmib: Parse error: Ignoring unknown option
'nodename=vmsrv01
```

27. Next, we have to browse the **HA** tab in the web interface and click on **Activate** to save the changes. In order to activate the changes, it is recommended to restart the `cman` and `pve-cluster` services.

28. In the next step, we need to include the cluster nodes in the *fencing domain for HA*. Edit the `/etc/default/redhat-cluster-pve` file with uncomment `FENCE_JOIN="yes"`. Restart the `cman` service and join *both the nodes* to fence the domain using the following command:

```
root@vmsrv01# /etc/init.d/cman restart
root@vmsrv01# fence_tool join
```

We are now ready to activate the HA function. The setup for this function is easy; just go to **Services**, find **RGManager**, and click on **Start** *on the top menu for both nodes*.

 If you cannot turn on the service at this stage, don't worry; the service will start when you configure an HA-enabled VM.

If you see that the RGManager has started in the **summary** page of **datacenter**, as shown in the following screenshot, it means that we were able to create HA-enabled VMs successfully!

Name	ID	Online	Suppor	Estranç	Server Address	Services
vmsrv01	1	Yes	-	No	192.168.1.57	PVECluster, RGManager
vmsrv02	2	Yes	-	No	192.168.1.58	PVECluster, RGManager

To automatically start the `rgmanager` service, issue the following command on both the nodes:

```
root@vmsrv01# update-rc.d rgmanager defaults
```

In the next section, I will show you the setup procedure of different storage options. You can choose one of them based on your system's configuration.

Building a Gluster filesystem for a Proxmox cluster

Instead of the network RAID 1 device formed by DRBD, we can also place our VMs into a Gluster filesystem.

As we have stated before, we will install three VMs with the CentOS platform for demonstration, based on the following network configuration:

Hostname	VM node	IP address	Subnet mask	Interface
glusterFS1	vmsrv01	192.168.1.51	255.255.255.0	vmbr0
glusterFS2	vmsrv02	192.168.1.52	255.255.255.0	vmbr0
glusterFS3	vmsrv03	192.168.1.53	255.255.255.0	vmbr0

For our practice, we set up three physical servers connected to the same network in which the Proxmox is located; we assign the vmbr0 interface (to know how to configure it, please refer to the network preparation section of this chapter) for them to use. I assume that you have already set up the hostname, IP configuration, and the /etc/hosts file.

 Each VM should have *at least 512 MB* memory installed.

After the network has been configured, we are ready to install the Gluster filesystem packages. Here, I will demonstrate the installation under the CentOS 6 platform; the latest stable version at the time of writing this book is 3.4.3-3, and the following steps will be applied to all of the three machines.

From http://download.gluster.org/pub/gluster/glusterfs/LATEST, download the following RPM packages: glusterfs, glusterfs-cli, glusterfs-fuse, glusterfs-libs, and glusterfs-server, and perform the following steps:

1. To install GlusterFS, we have to install the following libraries first:

   ```
   root# yum install openssl libaio-devel lvm2 xfsprogs
   ```

2. Before installing the GlusterFS package, install the libraries first:

   ```
   root# rpm -ivh glusterfs-libs-3.4.3-3.el6.x86_64.rpm
   ```

3. Next, install gluster-fuse, gluster-cli, and gluster-server with GlusterFS:

   ```
   root# rpm -ivh glusterfs-3.4.3-3.el6.x86_64.rpm \
   glusterfs-fuse-3.4.3-3.el6.x86_64.rpm \
   glusterfs-cli-3.4.3-3.el6.x86_64.rpm \
   glusterfs-server-3.4.3-3.el6.x86_64.rpm
   ```

   If you have encountered an error that tells you that rpcbind is needed for glusterfs-server, then you have to issue the following command to install the rpcbind service:

   ```
   Root# yum install rpcbind
   ```

4. If you cannot make the connection between nodes, set up the `iptable` firewall rules in each server to allow the incoming connections:

Server name	Iptable firewall rules
glusterFS1	`iptables -I INPUT -s 192.168.1.52 -j ACCEPT` `iptables -I INPUT -s 192.168.1.53 -j ACCEPT`
glusterFS2	`iptables -I INPUT -s 192.168.1.51 -j ACCEPT` `iptables -I INPUT -s 192.168.1.53 -j ACCEPT`
glusterFS3	`iptables -I INPUT -s 192.168.1.51 -j ACCEPT` `iptables -I INPUT -s 192.168.1.52 -j ACCEPT`

To make it simple, I have allowed transmission from other Gluster nodes. If it is not what you want, please make use of the following specifications to set up your own rules:

One port is reserved for each brick in a volume, starting from 24009 (for versions less than 3.4) and 49152 (for versions 3.4 and above). Ports 34865 to 34867 are reserved for the inline Gluster NFS server.

5. Then, we need to save the `iptables` configuration using the following command (optional):

```
root# service iptables save
```

6. Now, we start the Gluster daemon service using the following command:

```
root# /etc/init.d/glusterd start
```

7. Then, we configure the Gluster daemon to start on every boot using the following command:

```
root# chkconfig glusterd on
```

8. At the moment, no peer is set up, which can be checked using the following command:

```
root@glusterFS1# gluster peer status

peer status: No peers present
```

9. Add peer Gluster nodes (`glusterFS2` and `glusterFS3`) on `glusterFS1` using the following command:

```
root# gluster peer probe 192.168.1.52
root# gluster peer probe 192.168.1.53
```

10. We can check the peer status to confirm whether it is working or not using the following command:

```
root@glusterFS1# gluster peer status
Number of Peers: 2
Hostname: 192.168.1.12
...
Hostname 192.168.1.11
```

11. If the node is *not* in the `Peer in cluster` state, the node is not yet ready.

12. Then, we prepare a partition for the hard disk with the `fdisk` command and format it to XFS using the following command (assume we have the `/dev/vda1` *partiton*; if not, please create a new one with the `fdisk` command):

```
root# mkfs.xfs /etc/vda1
```

> XFS was the recommended filesystem for GlusterFS at the time of writing this book. We can also use EXT4 but it is not very stable. For more information on this, please refer to `http://www.gluster.org/community/documentation/index.php` and `https://lwn.net/Articles/544298/`.

13. If the command is not available in your machine, install the package using the following command:

```
root# apt-get install xfsprogs
```

14. Create a directory (`/glusterfs-data`) and mount point (`/glusterfs-data/mount1`) for the Gluster data nodes using the following command:

```
root# mount /dev/vda1 /glusterfs-data
root# mkdir -p /glusterfs-data/mount1
```

As we said, we need to make a subdirectory for Gluster use.

15. Edit `/etc/fstab` to make sure that the device is mounted on every boot:

```
/dev/vda1 /glusterfs-data xfs rw,user,auto  0  0
```

16. It's time to create our Gluster volume; type the following command in `GlusterFS1`:

```
root# gluster volume create glustertest replica 3 \
transport tcp 192.168.1.51:/glusterfs-data/mount1 \
192.168.1.52:/glusterfs-data/mount1 \
192.168.1.53:/glusterfs-data/mount1
```

17. Let's start the volume for use by using the following command:

```
root# gluster volume start glustertest
```

18. Then, you can check the volume status using the following command:

```
root# gluster volume info
Volume Name: glustertest
Type: Replicate
...
Bricks:
Brick1: 192.168.1.51:/glusterfs-data/mount1
Brick2: 192.168.1.52:/glusterfs-data/mount1
Brick3: 192.168.1.53:/glusterfs-data/mount1
```

19. Before adding volume to Proxmox, we need to add the following firewall rules:

```
root# iptables -I INPUT -s 192.168.1.57 -j ACCEPT
```

```
root# iptables -I INPUT -s 192.168.1.58 -j ACCEPT
```

```
root# service iptables save
```

20. If you are interested in tuning the performance for your GlusterFS volume, check the configurations in the master node (for example, glusterFS1) at the following location (optional): /var/lib/glusterd/vols/glustertest/trusted-glustertest-fuse.vol.

21. Make sure you stop the VMs that are running on Proxmox. Then, stop the Gluster volume in the Gluster master node with the following command (optional):

```
root@glusterFS1# gluster volume stop glustertest
```

22. You can add the following new options in the configuration file (optional):

```
Volume glustertest-write-behind
    type performance/write-behind
    option cache-size 3MB
    option flush-behind on
    subvolumes glustertest
end-volume
```

Parts of this code are explained as follows:

○ cache-size: This determines the total size of the write buffer used

○ flush-behind: This is used to increase the performance of handling lots of small files

23. After this, restart the volume named `glustertest` using the following command (optional):

```
root@glusterFS1# gluster volume start glustertest
```

 This is only one of the possible changes for performance; you can learn more at http://goo.gl/TwaKlo.

For more options on GlusterFS, visit http://goo.gl/N4j1JJ.

24. Next, we can add `glustertest` to our Proxmox server. Simply navigate to **Datacenter | Storage | Add | GlusterFS**. If the connection is okay, you should have the volume name suggestion, as shown in the following screenshot:

 By default, the Gluster server allows all clients to connect. If you cannot connect to the volume, you can modify the `auth.allow` option by using the following command:

```
root@glusterFS1# gluster volume set glustertest \
auth.allow 192.168.1.*
```

25. Unlike LVM, we can choose the content to be stored in this volume. Here, we choose **Images** for KVM and **Containers** for OpenVZ:

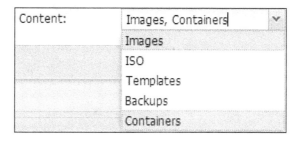

 Make sure the following four folders: `images`, `containers`, `vztmp`, and `dump` do not exist in your Gluster volume because Proxmox will try to create them and reject the use of the volume if this operation fails.

26. You should be able to view the volume information under the **glustertest** disk inside `vmsrv01` or `vmsrv02`, as shown in the following screenshot:

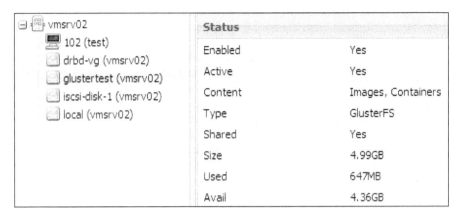

27. So, we can use the volume when building KVM VMs and OpenVZ containers. When we create the KVM VM, choose **glustertest** as storage, as shown in the following screenshot:

28. Similarly, when we create the OpenVZ container, **glustertest** is available for use, as shown in the following screenshot:

Now, we have created two new VMs with the following information:

Server ID	VM ID	VM name	VM type	IP	Storage
vmsrv01	203	gfs-kvm	KVM	192.168.2.13	glustertest
vmsrv01	204	gfs-vz	openVZ	192.168.2.14	glustertest

Based on your network quality, you might need to wait for a couple of minutes for the VM to be created. In the next section, we will go over another shared storage option—the Ceph filesystem.

Building a Ceph filesystem for a Proxmox cluster

We introduced the Ceph filesystem in *Chapter 3, Key Components for Building a Proxmox VE Cluster*, and we learned that it is a distributed filesystem. If you are not comfortable using the command line, Proxmox provides a built-in Ceph server service for you as an alternative option. Proxmox also provides a **GUI** to manage the Ceph service in its web management console, which should be much easier. In this section, I will show you how to build a Ceph service in Proxmox as a server and mount a Ceph device as a client.

As we mentioned before, we need to have three monitor nodes for a Ceph service. So, if we want to use Proxmox as a Ceph server, we need to have at least three nodes. Do you remember that we have already attached the network configuration for the third Proxmox server? Now, it's time for you to practice installing a Proxmox server and add it to the existing cluster. Remember to set up the hostname under the new node before adding it to the cluster. The following steps will guide you through building the Ceph filesystem:

1. If you have done everything well, you should be able to view a screen like this where the /dev/block/8:16 is the *quorum* disk we configured before:

2. Now, we can start installing Ceph support for Proxmox. With the Internet enabled, enter the following command on the three nodes:

```
root# pveceph install
```

3. Please pay attention, as it will take a while to download the necessary packages. When the installation is finished, simply issue the following command in vmsrv01:

```
root@vmsrv01# pveceph init --network 192.168.1.0/24
```

> The value of the network will be different based on the network configuration used for your Ceph storage. In our case, it is the Proxmox host node's infrastructure network.
>
> *Be aware that we need to use* pveceph *instead of the* ceph *command, as running the* ceph *command will generate a file not found error!*
>
> This configuration will be replicated to other nodes in the /etc/pve/ceph.conf file.

4. Next, we need to create a Ceph monitor with at least three or above nodes. If you want to install more than three nodes, make sure you have an odd number of monitors (for example, 3, 5, 7, and so on):

```
root@vmsrv01# pveceph createmon
```

5. After you have the first monitor, you can create the others via the web GUI. So we browse the Ceph tag (which is located at the end of the right-hand side) on the top menu under vmsvr01. Choose **Monitor** at the bottom to view the Ceph monitor page:

6. In the Ceph **Monitor** page, click on **Create**. Choose vmsrv02 and vmsrv03 accordingly, as shown in the following screenshot:

Name	Host	Quorum	Address
mon.1	vmsrv02	Yes	192.168.1.58:6789/0
mon.0	vmsrv01	Yes	192.168.1.57:6789/0
mon.2	vmsrv03	Yes	192.168.1.59:6789/0

7. After you finish adding the monitors, we are ready to add disks to the CephFS as **object storage devices** (OSD). Choose a single server from the *panel towards the left* that says vmsrv01. In the panel to the right, choose **ceph** from the *menu at the top*. Then, click on **Disks** at the *bottom*, and the hard drives connected to *vmsrv01* are displayed in the panel towards the right, as shown in the following screenshot:

Device	Usage	Size
/dev/sda	mounted	111.79GB
/dev/sdb	partitions	10.00GB
/dev/sdc	partitions	10.00GB
/dev/sdd	No	10.00GB
/dev/sde	No	10.00GB
/dev/sdf	osd.5	10.00GB

Status	Config	Monitor	Disks	OSD

Here, we have four types of usage status; the meaning of each is as follows:

- **Mounted**: This is used as the root device
- **Partitions**: This means that the drive is formatted with partitions
- **No**: This means that the drive is not formatted as a partition and is available to be used to form OSD
- **Osd.N**: This means the drive is created as the OSD volume

8. Thus, if you want to make Ceph storage on a *formatted* hard drive, make sure you have removed the partitions with the `fdisk` command. Choose an unused hard disk from the list and click on **Create: Ceph OSD**, as shown in the following command:

9. Accept the default setting and choose an SSD for the journal disk if you have one.

 The size of the OSD must be 10 GB or bigger.

10. After the configuration has completed, we will see a window similar to the following screenshot:

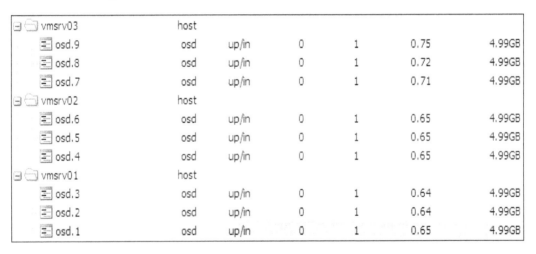

vmsrv03	host					
osd.9	osd	up/in	0	1	0.75	4.99GB
osd.8	osd	up/in	0	1	0.72	4.99GB
osd.7	osd	up/in	0	1	0.71	4.99GB
vmsrv02	host					
osd.6	osd	up/in	0	1	0.65	4.99GB
osd.5	osd	up/in	0	1	0.65	4.99GB
osd.4	osd	up/in	0	1	0.65	4.99GB
vmsrv01	host					
osd.3	osd	up/in	0	1	0.64	4.99GB
osd.2	osd	up/in	0	1	0.64	4.99GB
osd.1	osd	up/in	0	1	0.65	4.99GB

Currently, we have prepared our hard drives in Ceph, but we don't have any mount point for the client! To build a mount point for them, we need to create a *pool* under Ceph.

In any one of the Ceph nodes (vmsrv01 for example), we choose **pools** from the menu towards the bottom. Click on **create** present in the top menu, and the following window appears:

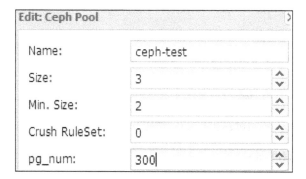

Here, we have defined the following options for our Ceph storage:

- **Name**: This is the mount point for the client connection.
- **Size**: This is used to set the number of replicas to be kept.
- **Min. Size**: This is used to set the minimum number of replicas to be kept.
- **Crush RuleSet**: It is okay to accept the default value, which is 0.
- **Pg_num**: This is used to set the number of placement groups for the pool, which is approximately 100 per OSD. It is calculated based on the following formula:

$$Total\ Placement\ Groups\ (PGs) = \frac{Number\ of\ OSDs\ *\ 100}{Number\ of\ Replicas}$$

In our case, this value is *(9*100) / 3 = 300*.

Mounting a Ceph device as shared storage

So far, we have built shared storage with Ceph but don't know how to use it on Proxmox. Let's see how we can use it:

1. To add a new storage to our cluster, again we have to click on **datacenter** in the panel towards the left, browse to **storage** in the panel towards the right, select **Add**, and choose **RBD**.

2. Then, we have to add our storage, as shown in the following screenshot:

The following are the options for RBD:

- **ID**: This is used to set the name for your storage in the cluster.
- **Pool** (ceph-test): This must be matched with the one we have configured before.
- **Monitor Host**: Add each Ceph monitor separated by a space, for example, 192.168.1.57 192.168.1.58 192.168.1.59 and so on.

3. However, after we have added the storage, you will see that the storage is not available and we cannot even know how much storage we are able to use:

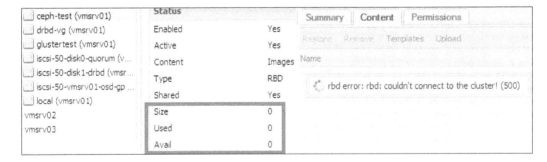

This is because we haven't copied the keyring file for the admin user while connecting the Ceph device. We have to create a new folder to store the keyring file before copying; for example, we copied the file from vmsrv01 in the following commands:

```
root@vmsrv01# mkdir /etv/pve/priv/ceph
root@vmsrv01# cp /etc/ceph/ceph.client.admin.keyring \ /etc/pve/priv/ceph/ceph-test.keyring
```

Notice that the keyring file is stored as follows:

```
/etc/pve/prive/ceph/<ceph_mountpoint_name>.keyring
```

4. Now, you should be able to view the content without any error, as shown in the following screenshot:

Status	
Enabled	Yes
Active	Yes
Content	Images
Type	RBD
Shared	Yes
Size	44.90GB
Used	364MB
Avail	44.55GB

As we are focusing on building a two-node cluster with Proxmox, I will not go further and test on the built-in CEPH storage.

We have gone through the setup procedures of different types of storage in Proxmox. Each storage option has its own advantages and disadvantages, so I would suggest that you test all of them to choose a suitable one. Meanwhile, I have prepared the following simple comparison between DRBD, GlusterFS, and CEPH for your reference when you need to choose your storage:

Product	DRBD	GlusterFS	CEPH
HDD size	2	N	N
Filesystem	EXT3, EXT4	EXT3, EXT4, and XFS	Its own system
Replication	Full	Full, diff, and reset	CRUSH
Management	CLI	CLI	GUI
Storage requirement	Partition-based	Directory-based	Partition-based

Based on the preceding table, I would suggest that you choose DRBD storage if you want to try it with the HA environment. For a production environment, it would be better to choose either GlusterFS or CEPH storage. Conceptually, GlusterFS would be easier to understand, but if you are not comfortable managing it with commands, then you can give CEPH a try.

Summary

In this chapter, a brief description of a cluster with HA was demonstrated. We also learned how to build shared storage as a quorum disk. With the help of the quorum disk, a two-node cluster was configured. Of course, the most important part of a cluster is the fencing devices. In our testing environment, we learned how to build them with the help of Cisco switches.

Besides that, we built our DRBD block device for VM migration, which will be shown to you in the next chapter. In the next chapter, we are going to build a VM that is protected under HA. Also, I am going to show you the behavior of our cluster during different levels of failure.

5
Testing on a Proxmox Cluster

In the previous chapter, we successfully built our own cluster system with Proxmox on both the two-node and three-node models. We also know that a quorum disk is essential for a two-node cluster to operate. But what if we have a node failure? What will happen to the cluster and how will it behave?

In this chapter, we are going to test whether our newly built cluster is protected by HA or not. To understand the whole picture of different scenarios, the testing will be conducted in both two-node and three-node clusters. Before we can begin our test, we have to make some changes to our DRBD storage. The key sections that will be covered in this chapter are as follows:

- Storage preparation for an LVM shared storage
- Demonstration of live migration for OpenVZ and KVM
- Building a VM with HA protection
- Testing different scenarios, including network failure, network switch failure, and cluster node failure

Storage preparation for an LVM shared storage

According to the *Installing and configuring DRBD* section in *Chapter 4, Configuring a Proxmox VE Cluster*, we have built an LVM volume with the /dev/sdc1 partition on both the Proxmox nodes to form our DRBD device. The /dev/sdc1 partition contains an LVM identifier on it as the LVM storage, and the LVM service tries to import it to the system; this might affect our DRBD mount point. It would be better to filter out this device to prevent any possible error by editing the /etc/lvm/lvm.conf file on both cluster nodes. Before we make any change to the file, we should back up the file with the following command:

```
root@vmsrv01# cp /etc/lvm/lvm.conf /etc/lvm/lvm.conf.bak
```

Then, we can make the following changes:

```
Original: filter = ["a/.*/" ]
New: filter = ["a|/dev/drbd1|", "r|/dev/sdc1|", "a/.*/" ]
```

In this example, we have defined the configuration, which is explained in the following points:

- `a|/dev/drbd1|`: This accepts LVM scanning on `/dev/drbd1`
- `r|/dev/sdc1|`: This rejects LVM scanning on `/dev/sdc1`
- `a/.*/`: This accepts LVM scanning on the remaining devices

Demonstration of live migration

What is the first benefit that we can enjoy after we have set up a Proxmox cluster? We are now able to perform live migration on our running VMs. Unlike offline migration, live migration allows you to have minimal downtime during the data migration from one cluster node to another.

Before moving on to the demonstration of live migration, do you remember that we created two VMs named VM 100 and VM 101 in *Chapter 1, Basic Concepts of a Proxmox Virtual Environment,* and two more VMs called VM 201, VM 202, VM 203, and VM 204 in *Chapter 4, Configuring a Proxmox VE Cluster?*

The following table shows the summary of the six VMs:

Host	VM ID	IP address	VM type	Storage type
vmsrv01	100	192.168.1.10	OpenVZ	Local
vmsrv01	101	192.168.1.11	KVM	Local
vmsrv01	201	192.168.2.11	KVM	DRBD
vmsrv01	202	192.168.2.12	OpenVZ	DRBD
vmsrv01	203	192.168.2.13	KVM	GlusterFS
vmsrv01	204	192.168.2.14	OpenVZ	GlusterFS

These VMs are being used to test the behavior when we perform a migration and configure the VMs with the HA environment. Now, we are going to test the operation of live migration on these VMs.

Using an OpenVZ container for live migration

Before starting with this section, we have to turn the VM on first. To test the availability, we will perform a simple *ping test from vmsrv01 to VM 100*. The following steps will guide you through this process:

1. We have to first get back to the web interface of Proxmox and check whether VM 100 is running under **vmsrv01**, as shown in the following screenshot:

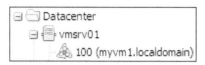

2. When we ping from **vmsrv01** to VM 100, the following results appear, which show that VM 100 is active:

```
PING 192.168.1.10 (192.168.1.10) 56(84) bytes of data.
64 bytes from 192.168.1.10: icmp_req=1 ttl=64 time=0.049 ms
64 bytes from 192.168.1.10: icmp_req=2 ttl=64 time=0.033 ms
```

3. It's time for us to test migrating a VM from vmsrv01 to vmsrv02. Right-click on **VM 100** and choose **Migrate**, set the **Target node** to **vmsrv02**, and check the **Online** option for live migration, as shown in the following screenshot:

4. Before clicking on the **Migrate** button, we have to keep checking the status of **VM 100** using the ping test to ensure that the service is not interrupted. In the task history, we can find that the container is moving, as shown in the following output:

```
starting migration of CT 100 to node 'vmsrv02' (192.168.1.58)
container is running - using online migration
starting rsync phase 1
/usr/bin/rsync -aHAX --delete --numeric-ids --sparse \
/var/lib/vz/private/100 root@192.168.1.58:/var/lib/vz/private
dump container state
copy dump file to target node
starting rsync (2nd pass)
/usr/bin/rsync -aHAX --delete --numeric-ids \
```

```
/var/lib/vz/private/100 root@192.168.1.58:/var/lib/vz/private
dump 2nd level quota
copy 2nd level quota to target node
initialize container on remote node 'vmsrv02'
initializing remote quota
turn on remote quota
load 2nd level quota
starting container on remote node 'vmsrv02'
restore container state
removing container files on local node
start final cleanup
migration finished successfully (duration 00:01:49)
```

At first, the Proxmox server will initiate the `vzmigrate` command and pass the `--online` option to the server to indicate that it is an online migration. From the operation log, we found that live migration is making use of the `rsync` command to copy files under the OpenVZ container directory to the target cluster node.

Two `rsync` operations are run. The first time, it tries to copy all data from the OpenVZ container with the `--sparse` command-line option that will reduce the used space at the destination side.

Then, the second time, the `rsync` operation tries to copy the current state and memory map to a destination node for restoration. From the output log, we found that the OpenVZ container is *suspended* once the migration process starts. As the container is suspended during the migration process, we will suffer from a period of downtime in proportion to the amount of memory allocated to the VMs. Therefore, if we need to move the OpenVZ container on a production platform, we must take such downtime into consideration.

```
Reply from 192.168.1.10: bytes=32 time=24ms TTL=63
Reply from 192.168.1.57: Destination host unreachable.
Reply from 192.168.1.58: Destination host unreachable.
Reply from 192.168.1.58: Destination host unreachable.
Reply from 192.168.1.10: bytes=32 time=2ms TTL=63
```

From the ping test result, we found that the container is not available for a duration of three ping packets, and the respondent is transferred from `vmsrv01(192.168.1.57)` to `vmsrv02(192.168.1.58)` during the operation. How about if we move an OpenVZ container to a DRBD storage? Let's check if there is any difference by performing the following steps:

1. Perform the same steps as mentioned earlier, but this time, we choose **VM 202**.

2. Then, we can check the system log; you should see something similar to the following output:

```
container is running - using online migration
starting rsync phase 1...
start live migration - suspending container
starting rsync (2nd pass)...
migration finished successfuly (duration 00:01:45)
```

The operation is the same as what we did in the previous section because the DRBD storage for our OpenVZ container is a local storage only. So, there is no difference during a system migration between VM 100 and VM 202. How about if we try to migrate an OpenVZ container using the GlusterFS storage? The following steps will show you how to do this:

1. Perform the same steps as you did earlier, but this time, choose **VM 204**.

2. Then, check the system log; you should have an output similar to the following output:

```
starting migration of CT 204 to node 'vmsrv02' (192.168.1.58)
container is running - using online migration
container data is on shared storage 'glustertest'
start live migration - suspending container
dump container state
dump 2nd level quota
initialize container on remote node 'vmsrv02'
initializing remote quota
turn on remote quota
load 2nd level quota
starting container on remote node 'vmsrv02'
restore container state
start final cleanup
migration finished successfully (duration 00:06:38)
```

We found that Proxmox *skipped the two-level* rsync *operation* and simply dumped the container state and quota from the source to the destination, because the container is stored in shared storage. Therefore, there is no need to copy the files again and check whether the *source VM data is removed*. Next, let's take a look at the migration process using a KVM.

Live migration with a KVM

Again, we start our testing with a KVM that is not running in shared storage; here, we have VM 101. Before we turn this VM on for testing, we need to remove the extra configurations rather than the VM root drive itself, for example, an extra hard disk drive, a CD-ROM device mounted with an ISO image, and so on. If you have just finished the installation of the OS on VM 101, we might have a CD-ROM device mounted with a physical drive or ISO file. The following steps will guide you through the migration process:

1. To remove the mounted drive setting, click on **VM 101** on the panel on the left-hand side and choose **Hardware** on the panel on the right-hand side. Check the value of **CD/DVD Drive**; make sure that it is set to **Do not use any media**, as shown in the following screenshot:

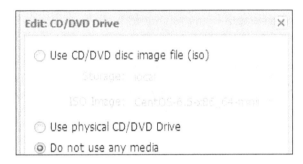

   Then, we will notice that the configuration has changed, as shown in the following screenshot:

2. After we have finished changing the settings, we can now turn on the machine, right-click on it, and choose **Migrate**. As usual, we use the **online** option for live migration. Unlike the OpenVZ container, the live migration for **VM 101** fails. The following process log shows that because the disk image is not stored in shared storage, the operation fails:

```
starting migration of VM 101 to node 'vmsrv02' (192.168.1.58)
copying disk images
...
ERROR: migration aborted (duration 00:00:00): Failed to sync
data - can't do online migration - VM uses local disks
```

We cannot perform live migration on a KVM with local storage.

3. So, we are going to use the KVM that was created in *Chapter 4, Configuring a Proxmox VE Cluster*, with VM 201. Note that we also need to remove extra configurations such as the mounted CD-ROM, ISO files, and so on. Here is our expected output:

```
starting migration of VM 201 to node 'vmsrv02' (192.168.1.58)
copying disk images
starting VM 201 on remote node 'vmsrv02'
starting ssh migration tunnel
starting online/live migration on localhost:60000
migrate_set_speed: 8589934592
migrate_set_downtime: 0.1
migration speed: 256.00 MB/s - downtime 3 ms
migration status: completed
migration finished successfully (duration 00:00:12)
```

As compared to the live migration under an OpenVZ container, there is only a 3 ms downtime during the live migration under the KVM. Why is the system migration for a KVM performed so fast? Here are the reasons:

- The KVM will not be suspended at the beginning of the migration process; this reduces the downtime

- The KVM uses a pre-copy memory migration that was mentioned in *Chapter 2, Getting Started with a High Availability (HA) Environment,* which will only stop the source VM after copying most of the memory map data

- As the VM is stored in shared storage, not a lot of data is needed to be copied

Let's see the ping test result for the KVM live migration:

```
42 packets transmitted, 42 received, 0% packet loss
```

Now, we have tested migration with one of the most important functions of a Proxmox cluster. In the next part, we will protect our VMs using HA.

Building an HA-protected VM

In *Chapter 1, Basic Concepts of a Proxmox Virtual Environment*, we created two VMs with OpenVZ and KVM (VM 100 and VM 101, respectively) for demonstration purposes. As they are stored locally, they do not have the HA ability. So, we have to use VM 201 and VM 202, which were created in *Chapter 4, Configuring a Proxmox VE Cluster*, for testing. The following steps will guide you in building an HA-protected VM:

1. Make sure that you have enabled the resource group manager (`rgmanager`) service (refer to *Chapter 4, Configuring a Proxmox VE Cluster*, if you don't know how to enable them), as shown in the following screenshot:

Name	ID	Online	Support	Estranged	Server Address	Services
vmsrv01	1	Yes	-	No	192.168.1.57	PVECluster, RGManager
vmsrv02	2	Yes	-	No	192.168.1.58	PVECluster, RGManager

2. First, *turn off the VMs before applying the HA-protected configuration*. Then, choose the `Datacenter` folder from the panel on the left-hand side and find the **HA** tab. You should see a screen similar to the following screenshot:

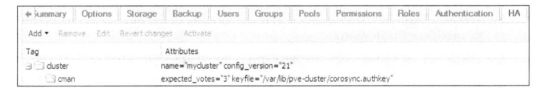

3. Navigate to **Add | HA managed VM/CT | Create: HA managed VM/CT**, as shown in the following screenshot:

4. Enter `201` as the **VMID**, and select the **Auto Start** option. Then, click on the **Create** button. This action will make changes to the `cluster.conf` file. To confirm the change, we click on the **Activate** button on the top menu. If everything is working fine, you will see that a small section of code is inserted in the `cluster.conf` file, as shown in the following screenshot:

 Your VM will *not be able to perform offline migration* if it is HA-protected!

The preceding setting is simply telling the Resource Group Manager (**RGManager**) that there is a VM that should be under its management whose **VMID** is **201**.

5. If we go back to the **Summary** page under **Datacenter**, the VM with a VMID equal to 201 has been added to the HA service, but the status is **disabled**.

HA Service Status			
Name	Owner	Status	Restarts
pvevm:201	none	disabled	0

6. After that, we can start the VM. The Proxmox cluster performs a different start up process, as shown in the following screenshot:

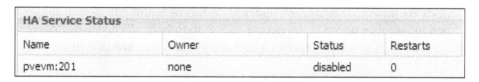

Node	User name	Description	Status	
vmsrv01	root@pam	HA 201 - Start	OK	with HA protected
vmsrv01	root@pam	VM 201 - Start	OK	normal startup

7. Also, the status of the HA service for our VM is changed to **started**, as shown in the following screenshot:

HA Service Status			
Name	Owner	Status	Restarts
pvevm:201	vmsrv01	started	0

As we cannot use the `vmctl start <VMID>` command anymore, we need to use a new command called `clusvcadm` with an `-e` option to enable the HA service:

```
root@vmsrv01# clusvcadm -e pvevm:<VMID>
```

Now, we have built a VM with HA. Before we move on, we can check out some of the new terms used in this section:

- **Resource Group Manager (RGManager)**: This combines with the **cluster manager (CMAN)** and **distributed lock manager (DLM)** processes to manage and provide failover capabilities for the collection of resources called services, resource groups, or resource trees. It is an essential process for HA on services. If this service is turned off, the HA function is disabled.

- **Cluster manager (CMAN)**: As the name implies, this is the main process of the cluster architecture. CMAN manages the state of quorum the status of different cluster members. In order to check the status of all the cluster members, *monitoring messages are sent periodically to all cluster nodes*. If there is any status change on the cluster member, it will be distributed to the remaining cluster nodes.

  It is also responsible for *quorum management*. When more than half of the node members are active, a cluster is said to be *healthy*. If the number of active member nodes is decreased to less than half, *all cluster-related activities are blocked*. A few more features that are not allowed are as follows::

  - Any change made to the `cluster.conf` file is not allowed
  - You'll not be able to start the resource manager; this disables the HA function
  - Any operation to create a VM is blocked

   The operation of the existing VMs without HA are not affected.

- **Distributed lock manager (DLM)**: This is used by the resource group manager to apply different lock modes to resources to prevent multiple accesses. For details, refer to `http://en.wikipedia.org/wiki/Distributed_lock_manager`.

I have prepared a simple diagram that shows the relationship between the terms described previously:

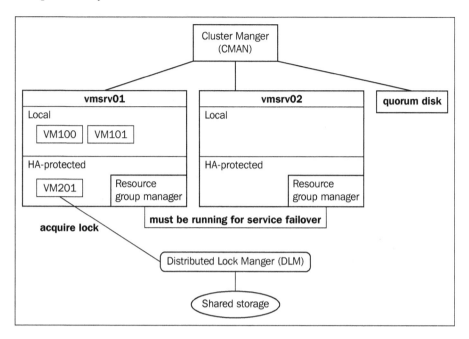

Of course, we would like to add HA to an OpenVZ container too. Therefore, we follow the steps to configure an HA-protected VM, as demonstrated earlier. If you have done everything that is needed, you should have the following two entries under the HA-service status section:

HA Service Status		
Name	Owner	Status
pvevm:201	none	disabled
pvevm:202	none	disabled

In this section, we have successfully created an HA-protected VM under both the OpenVZ and KVM environments. Next, we will try to test whether our HA environment is working or not.

Testing with the cluster environment

We have gone through one of the most important features provided by a Proxmox cluster. Under HA protection, the VMs are supposed to be online until there is not enough quorum in a cluster. At this stage, I would like to test the cluster functionality first by relocating the VM from one node to another.

Testing an HA service relocation

As a starting point, we need to ensure that the VM can be started up in both the Proxmox nodes. As the VM is HA-protected, we cannot use `vzctl start` for OpenVZ containers and `qm start` for KVM machines. Instead, we use `clusvcadm` with the `-e` option in the following format:

```
root@vmsrv01# clusvcadm -e pvevm:<VMID>
```

 In this command, `pvevm` is used as a prefix to indicate that it is an HA-protected VM.

What if we need to relocate the HA service from one node to another? We use the following command:

```
root@vmsrv01# clusvcadm -r pvevm:<VMID> <proxmox_node>
```

Testing the OpenVZ container relocation

In the previous chapter, we created three different OpenVZ containers, but the one with local storage is not available, so the possible containers are:

- VM 202 with the `drbd-ext4` storage
- VM 204 with the `glustertest` storage

We will try to test them one by one. First, we will test VM 202 using the following steps:

1. Relocate an OpenVZ container (VM 202) using the following command:
   ```
   root@vmsrv01# clusvcadm -r pvevm:202 vmsrv02
   ```
   We find that the VM cannot be relocated, and we get the following error code:

Node	User name	Description	Status
vmsrv02	root@pam	CT 202 - Start	OK
vmsrv01	root@pam	CT 202 - Start	Error: command 'vzctl start 202' failed: exit code 62
vmsrv02	root@pam	CT 202 - Shutdown	OK

If we look at the error log, we find that the destination node cannot find the data for the VM:

```
task started by HA resource agent
Starting container ...
stat(/drbd-store/ext4/private/202): No such file or directory
Can't umount /var/lib/vz/root/202: Invalid argument
```

This is because the container is not stored in shared storage; this causes the relocation to fail.

2. So, we add VM 204 to be managed by the HA service and start the service with the following command:

   root@vmsrv01# clusvcadm -e pvevm:204

3. Then, we try to relocate the VM to vmsrv02 with the following command:

   root@vmsrv01# clusvcadm -r pvevm:204 vmsrv02

4. The process log is different from the VM 202 relocation; there is no error now.

Node	User name	Description	Status
vmsrv02	root@pam	CT 204 - Start	OK
vmsrv01	root@pam	CT 204 - Shutdown	OK

These steps show that shared storage is essential for an OpenVZ container relocation. Of course, we also want to check the behavior of a KVM relocation, too.

Testing a KVM relocation

Just like the OpenVZ container, we cannot add a VM with local storage to the HA environment, so we can choose from our existing VMs:

- VM 201 with the drbd-vg storage
- VM 203 with the glustertest storage

Now, we will try to test the behavior of different storages in KVM:

1. Make sure that the VM is running; then, perform relocation with the following commands:

   root@vmsrv01# clusvcadm -e pvevm:201

   root@vmsrv01# clusvcadm -r pvevm:201 vmsrv02

2. There should be no problem at all, as shown in the **Status** column of the following screenshot:

Node	User name	Description	Status
vmsrv02	root@pam	VM 201 - Start	OK
vmsrv01	root@pam	VM 201 - Shutdown	OK

3. We can test VM 203 with the following command:

```
root@vmsrv01# clusvcadm -r pvevm:203 vmsrv02
```

4. We have a similar output result for VM 203 relocation:

Node	User name	Description	Status
vmsrv02	root@pam	VM 203 - Start	OK
vmsrv01	root@pam	VM 203 - Shutdown	OK

As we can see, Proxmox tries to shut down the VM from source and then starts it up at the destination node. Therefore, we can only minimize the downtime but cannot reach zero downtime for both OpenVZ containers and KVMs.

Testing a single network interface failure

In order to meet the requirements of an HA cluster, it should be able to bear different levels of failures without service interruption. Let's perform a simple ping test on network failures in a cluster node.

First, we will test whether our system is operational if there is a single network card failure. For simulation, we will turn off one network interface on vmsrv01 and start up a ping test from vmsrv02 to see what will happen.

Issue the ping command from vmsrv02 to test the connectivity of vmsrv01:

```
root@vmsrv02# ping 192.168.1.57
```

Now, turn off the network interface (eth0) from vmsrv01:

```
root@vmsrv01# ifconfig eth0 down
```

In our expectation, the connectivity of vmsrv01 should not be affected because we have created a bonding device (bond0) with the failover policy and assigned the IP address 192.168.1.57 to it. Let's check the output we got from the ping test:

```
64 bytes from 192.168.1.57: icmp_req=536 ttl=64 time=0.353 ms
...
560 packets transmitted, 560 received, 0% packet loss
```

Here, I tested it for over 500 packets and found no packet loss during the ping test. Now, we need to check the status in the graphic interface by browsing to https://192.168.1.57:8006. In the cluster summary, **vmsrv01** is still marked as **Online**, as shown in the following screenshot:

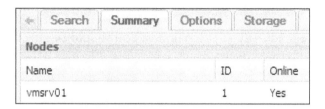

From this screenshot, we can say that our cluster has passed the availability test. Before we move on to the next test, make sure that you have rolled back the change by logging in to vmsrv01 and issuing the following command:

```
root@vmsrv01# ifconfig eth0 up
```

Testing a single network switch failure

In this section, we are going to create a test to simulate a network switch failure. To avoid network inaccessibility between two switches, we have to add an extra switch—**Switch A**—before we can actually turn the switch off. A diagram of the connection is shown as follows:

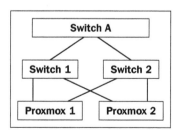

The following steps will help you check the status of your connections:

1. When two switches are available, we can check the status of the bonding device using the following command:

```
root# cat /proc/net/bond/bond0

Bonding Mode: fault-tolerance (active-backup)
Currently Active Slave: eth0
Slave Interface: eth0
MII Status: up
Slave Interface: eth1
MII Status: up
```

2. Next, we can simply power off the switch and watch its impact on our cluster. After we have confirmed that the switch is powered off, we can check the /var/log/message file on both nodes. You should be able to see that the connection for *eth0 is down*, and the bonding interface will switch to use eth1 as the *primary* device:

```
vmsrv02 kernel: eth0: link down
vmsrv02 kernel: bonding: bond0: link status definitely down for
interface eth0, disabling it
vmsrv02 kernel: bonding: bond0: making interface eth1 the new
active one.
```

3. Inside the status of the bonding device, the interface state for eth0 changes to down, as shown in the following output:

```
Slave Interface: eth0
MII Status: down
```

So, we have proven that the availability of our cluster nodes is not affected by a single switch failure. Let's move on to see whether the cluster will be disabled in the case of a failed cluster node.

Testing a single cluster node failure

In the previous sections, we tested the different types of network failures that can cause the cluster to become unusable. Fortunately, with the configuration we have applied, our cluster can still operate in a tough environment.

As we have two running HA-enabled VMs (that is, VM 201 and VM 202), we can simply fence `vmsrv02` to test how Proxmox handles HA VMs if the corresponding cluster node has been shut down:

root@vmsrv01# fence_node vmsrv02

The services that run in vmsrv02 have all *failed*. This is not our expectation and not acceptable! When there is a node failure (for example, system reboot, shutdown, or hardware failure), the VMs configured with the HA protection should be migrated to other healthy nodes. Why would this problem occur? This will occur as we do not configure a failover domain that tells Proxmox what to do when there is a node failure.

Setting up a failover domain

According to the definition in Red Hat, a failover domain is a named subset of cluster nodes that are eligible to run a cluster service in the event of a node failure. This means that if there is a node failure, the nodes inside the subset will take the place and responsibility of the failed member that will move the VM to the other node, in our case. For more information, refer to `http://goo.gl/6Vmbjb`.

At the time of writing this book, we have to configure a failover domain under CLI by adding new settings to the `cluster.conf` file.

You might notice that there is a **Failover domain** option under the **Add** button on the HA-management page. However, if you choose it, you will get the following window, which shows you that there is no GUI tool available yet:

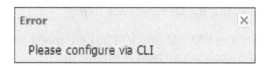

The steps required to set up a failover domain are as follows:

1. First, we need to copy the current contents of the `cluster.conf` file to form a new file named `cluster.conf.new`:

   root# cp /etc/pve/cluster.conf /etc/pve/cluster.conf.new

2. Assume that the current version for the configuration file is 59. Before we make any changes to the configuration file, increment `config_version` by 1, which becomes 60, in the `/etc/pve/cluster.conf.new` file:

   ```
   <cluster config_version="60" name="mycluster">
   ```

3. Then, we need to add the failover domain section after the `rm` tag and before the `pvevm` tag:

```
</rm>
  <failoverdomains>
    <failoverdomain name="myfailover" nofailback="1" ordered="1"
      restricted="1">
        <failoverdomainnode name="vmsrv01" priority="1"/>
        <failoverdomainnode name="vmsrv02" priority="2"/>
    </failoverdomain>
  </failoverdomains>
<pvevm>
```

First, we defined `restricted` (`restricted="1"`) and `ordered` (`ordered="1"`) in the failover domain named `myfailover` without setting `failback` (`nofailback="0"`). Besides, we have to check whether the recovery method of our VM is set to `"relocate"`. The meanings of these settings can be summarized as follows:

- ○ **Restricted domain**: This means we only make use of defined failover nodes when a failover is needed.

- ○ **Ordered domain** (`nofailback="1"` and `recovery="relocate"`): This means that priority is applied to the cluster node. A service is relocated to another cluster node when its owner is down. With the `nofailback` setting equaling 1, if the priority of the original service owner is higher than the relocated one, then the service will *not* be relocated back to its original owner when it comes back online. This allows the system administrator to check the failed cluster node before moving the services back to it.

4. After that, changes to VM 203 and VM 204 are made to identify what kind of action is needed if their active host is turned off:

```
<pvevm autostart="1" vmid="203" domain="myfailover"
recovery="relocate"/>
<pvevm autostart="1" vmid="204" domain="myfailover"
recovery="relocate"/>
```

5. Finally, remember to *close the rm tag* by adding the following code after the previous lines of code:

```
</rm>
```

6. Save this file. Click on **Datacenter** on the panel on the left-hand side in the web console and find the **HA** tab on the panel on the right-hand side. Click on **Activate** to make new changes.

7. Now, we have configured a higher priority value for vmsrv02. Therefore, we expect that the VM203 and VM204 services will be relocated back to vmsrv02 when it comes online. We can test the failover function by fencing vmsrv02 using the following command:

```
root@vmsrv01 # fence_node vmsrv02
```

8. Now, VM 203 and VM 204 are still not available after vmsrv02 is fenced. Here is the ping test result for them:

```
64 bytes from 192.168.1.21: icmp_req=33 ttl=64 time=0.52 ms
From 192.168.1.57 icmp_seq=67 Destination Host Unreachable
...
64 bytes from 192.168.1.22: icmp_req=29 ttl=64 time=0.30 ms
From 192.168.1.57 icmp_seq=63 Destination Host Unreachable
```

9. Instead of keeping the services down, after around half a minute, the services are relocated to vmsrv01, as shown in the following screenshot:

HA Service Status					
Name ▼	Owner	Status	Restarts	Last transition	Last owner
pvevm:204	vmsrv01	started	0	Mon May 19 2014 06:48:49 GMT+08...	vmsrv02
pvevm:203	vmsrv01	started	0	Mon May 19 2014 06:48:49 GMT+08...	vmsrv02

Why do we have downtime for half a minute? This is because we have defined 30000 microseconds as the *value of the totem token*, which equals 30 seconds, for the waiting time of a heartbeat message in the *Forming a two-node cluster with DRBD* section of *Chapter 4, Configuring a Proxmox VE Cluster*. Therefore, we need to wait for 30 seconds before determining whether vmsrv02 is down, as shown in the following steps:

1. To restore the status of vmsrv02, issue the following command in vmsrv01:

```
root@vmsrv01# fence_node vmsrv02 -U
```

2. We also need to transit the services back to vmsrv02 using the following command:

```
root@vmsrv01# clusvcadm -r pvevm:201
root@vmsrv01# clusvcadm -r pvevm:202
```

Summary

In this chapter, we have gone through two important features of Proxmox—live migration and HA. Using live migration, we can shift our services to other machines with minimal system downtime when we find that the system resources on a cluster node are almost fully utilized. This allows us to have better resource management. With a VM running with HA, the system downtime can be minimized, and the system administrators are not required to monitor the system 24/7 on their own.

In the next chapter, we are going to see how to import our existing operating systems to our Proxmox cluster to enjoy the functionalities we just mentioned.

6

System Migration of an Existing System to a Proxmox VE Cluster

In *Chapter 5, Testing on a Proxmox Cluster*, we did some tests on our Proxmox cluster. During our tests, the VMs under HA protection were not affected due to a network card or a network switch failure. Even if we manually turned off one cluster node, the VMs where HA was enabled will automatically be switched to the remaining nodes.

Building a VM from scratch is pretty easy, but what if we already have a running system in hand? In this chapter, we are going to demonstrate the processes of moving an existing system to our cluster platform. The following topics will be covered in this chapter:

- System migration of an existing Linux platform
- Live migration of a physical machine to a KVM
- System migration of a Windows platform
- System migration from VMware to Proxmox
- System migration from XenServer / Hyper-V Server to Proxmox

Assume we have a physical machine with the following system specifications:

- **OS**: CentOS 6.5 and the Windows Server 2012 standard edition.
- **CPU**: Any CPU with two physical cores.
- **Memory**: 1 GB RAM for Linux, and 2 GB RAM for Windows.

- **Hard drive**: For Linux, a 10 GB hard drive is required with two LVM volumes—lv_root and lv_swap.

  For Windows, a 20 GB hard drive is needed with one hidden system volume and one data volume.

- **NIC**: One network card with the IP address ranging from 192.168.1.31 to 37 with the subnet mask 255.255.255.0 is required. A temporary IP address, 192.168.1.39, will be used during the migration.

- For VMware system migration, VMware ESXi Version 5.5 is used.

- For XenServer system migration, XenServer Version 6.2 is used.

Our demonstration assumes that you only have one physical hard drive and one physical network adapter. If you have multiple hard drives, and you have created multiple mount points under your physical machine, you have to add the same number of virtual disk drives and customize the /etc/fstab file under your VM so as to make the migration successful.

If we move the Linux platform to form an OpenVZ container, please note that for most circumstances, migrating the current system to KVM-based VMs requires the existing system to shut down while we do the live migration.

System migration of an existing Linux platform

This type of migration can only be used for a Linux platform and has a limit of only one hard drive as an OpenVZ container does not allow you to add extra hard drives.

Preparing for container migration on a Proxmox server

We have two different approaches to do the system migration. These have been explained in the following points:

1. You can simply perform an rsync operation from the source machine on the Proxmox server, and then create a configuration file for the OpenVZ container.

2. You can create a blank container and copy the data from the source. You can view the link http://goo.gl/byzsji for your reference.

If we start our migration with the template file, we are likely to run into trouble for comparing the files on the source and destination machines, because the target container will also contain the data copied from the template. Therefore, it is much better to create the container using the GUI, keeping the configuration files, and remove all the data inside. The following steps will guide you in creating the container:

1. Click on the **Create CT** button at the top right and fill in the following information:

 The password will be overwritten by the source machine.

2. For the **Template** tab, make sure you have downloaded the OpenVZ template file for the required Linux distribution and OS version from http://wiki.openvz.org/Download/template/precreated.

3. *This is the most important step!* To reduce the chance of having a hardware problem, make sure that you allocate enough system resources (similar to the source machine):

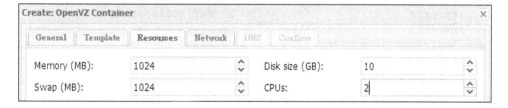

4. For the network part, we choose **venet** and enter the IP address (for example, 192.168.1.31) for the VM.

5. The DNS settings are not important; you can use the following example:
    ° DNS domain: localdomain
    ° DNS Server 1: 192.168.1.1

6. When the operation completes, make sure you turn off the newly created VM. Then, double-confirm if the OSTEMPLATE option is already set up in the `/etc/vz/conf/301.conf` file:

```
OSTEMPLATE="centos-6-x86_64_minimal.tar.gz"
```

Our preparation process is now complete. In the next section, we are going to copy data from the source machine to our VM using the `rsync` command.

Migrating data to a container using the rsync command

In order to ensure that all our data is properly copied even with minor data changes, we have to perform the `rsync` operation twice. In the first pass, most of the data is copied from the source while minor changes will be copied in the second pass when we turn off most of the system services (for example, web, database, mail, and so on). With such an approach, the system downtime is minimized.

Before we can proceed with copying, make sure that the `rsync` command is available on both the machines and perform the following steps (*all the commands should be executed from vmsrv01 unless advised*):

1. First, we have to create a list of directories that are to be excluded during the copy operation because the environment for a virtual platform is different from the physical one. If we copy the information directly from the source, our VM might be unable to start up. So, we create a file with the following code under `/tmp/exclude.txt`:

```
/tmp        # folder containing temporary files
/boot       # boot folder, stores information used for booting up
/lib/modules# library modules
/etc/blkid  # stores information about block devices
/etc/mtab   # stores information on currently mounted FS
/etc/lvm    # stores information for LVM devices
/etc/fstab  # stores information on mount points
/etc/udev   # stores naming alias for devices
```

2. We have to allow remote access for the root account *in the physical machine*. Edit the `/etc/ssh/sshd_config` file to enable the PermitRootLogin option:

```
PermitRootLogin yes
```

3. Restart the SSH service *of the physical machine* to apply the configuration changes:

```
service sshd restart
```

4. Next, we can start copying the files from the source to the destination:

```
[root@vmsrv01]# rsync -avz -A -H --one-file-system --numeric-ids \
--exclude-from=/tmp/exclude.txt root@192.168.1.31:/ \
/var/lib/vz/private/301
```

If you have defined a customized port for the SSH server, you have to tweak the command, as follows:

```
[root@vmsrv01]# rsync -e "ssh -p <ssh_port> -i <identity> -avz -A
-H --one-file-system --numeric-ids --exclude-from="/tmp/exclude.
txt" root@192.168.1.31:/ /var/lib/vz/private/301
```

 Make sure that you have entered the command in a single line.

5. Configure the network interface to ensure that the IP settings are applied:

```
[root@vmsrv01]# vzctl set 301 –ipadd 192.168.1.31 –save
```

As the container is different from a physical machine, we have to make the modifications under the Proxmox server using the following commands:

```
Line1: cd /var/lib/vz/private/301
Line2: sed -i -e 's/^[0-9].*getty.*tty/#&/g' etc/inittab
Line3: ln -sf /proc/mounts etc/mtab
Line4: mv etc/fstab etc/fstab.old
Line5: egrep '/dev/pts|/dev/shm|/proc|/sys' etc/fstab.old >
       etc/fstab
Line6: mknod --mode 666 dev/ptmx c 5 2
Line7: mkdir -p dev/pts
Line8: cp -a /dev/ttyp* /dev/ptyp* dev
Line9: /sbin/MAKEDEV -d dev ttyp ptyp
Line10: rm -rf dev/null
Line11: mknod --mode 666 dev/null c 1 3
Line12: mknod --mode 444 dev/urandom c 1 9
Line13: mkdir proc
Line14: cp -a etc/network/interfaces etc/network/interfaces.old
Line15: cat /dev/null > etc/network/interfaces
```

These commands are explained as follows:

- In line 1, we have navigated to the directory of the container.
- In line 2, as the container does not contain real ttys, we have to disable the getty content inside/etc/inittab.

- In line 3, we linked the {VMDIR}/etc/mtab file to /proc/mounts with the host system (that is, Proxmox). The container's root filesystem (/) is not actually mounted at root (/); rather, it is under the host's filesystem. Therefore, linking the mount file from the host system to the VM will make the df command work properly in a VM.

- In lines 4 and 5, we create a backup of the /etc/fstab file first. Since the container does not have a real hard disk, there should be no entries except /dev/pts, /proc, and /sys.

- In lines 6 to 9, we are trying to create tty device nodes for the vzctl command to work. The directories included are /dev/ptmx, /dev/pts/, /dev/ttyp*, and /dev/ptyp*.

  If you cannot use the MAKEDEV command, you can copy the file directly with the following command:

  ```
  cp -a /dev/ttyp* /dev/ptyp* /var/lib/vz/private/301/dev/
  ```

- In lines 10 and 11, we make sure that /dev/null is correctly configured. So, we remove the old one and create a new one with the mknod command.

- In line 12, we create /dev/urandom for a random generator; please refer to http://www.2uo.de/myths-about-urandom/ for more info about random generators.

- In line 13, we create the /proc directory if it does not exist. This folder is used to store runtime system information. For more details on system information, you can check out http://goo.gl/Q0917w.

- In lines 14 and 15, we copied the network configuration files for the VM.

6. The VM is now ready for us to start testing; issue the following commands:

```
[root@vmsrv01]# vzctl start 301
[root@vmsrv01]# vzctl enter 301
```

7. If the VM is working as expected, turn off the source machine and turn on the network interface inside the newly-created container with the following command:

```
[root@p2v-01]# ifconfig eth0 up
```

If you are using Fedora, your network interface might be venet0, so the command becomes:

```
[root@p2v-01]# ifconfig venet0 up
```

The downtime for system migration to an OpenVZ container for a Linux platform is minimum in our demonstration; this is because the OpenVZ container shares the Linux kernel with the host system. So, if the kernel version of your source system cannot run on the Linux kernel that Proxmox is using, you may need to use a KVM-based VM. In the next section, we will cover the procedures of system migration to form a KVM-based VM.

Live migration of a physical machine to a KVM

Such a migration will only work for a Linux platform. Let's check how we can convert our Linux platform to a virtualized one.

Preparing for migration on the source machine

Make sure that logging in from the root account is allowed via SSH on the physical server (as the data source) and vmsrv01, just as we did while migrating the system from a physical machine to an OpenVZ container. To make it simpler, I will create a folder named /backup to store the backup files. Make sure that you have enough disk space to place a backup of your boot partition. The following steps will guide you through the process of migration:

1. Create a backup folder in both the physical machine and vmsrv01:

   ```
   mkdir /backup
   ```

2. Check the partition name used by Linux to boot up the system from the source machine using the following command:

   ```
   [root@source]# fdisk -l
   Disk /dev/sda: 10.7 GB, 10737418240 bytes
   ...
   Device    Boot      Start         End      Blocks   Id  System
   /dev/sda1    *           1          64      512000   83  Linux
   Partition 1 does not end on cylinder boundary.
   /dev/sda2               64        1306     9972736   8e  Linux LVM

   [root@source]# cat /etc/fstab
   /dev/mapper/vg_p2v01-lv_root / ext4 defaults 11
   /dev/mapper/vg_p2v01-lv_swap swap       swap      defaults        0 0
   ```

From this output result, we know the following information:

- ○ /dev/sda1 is our *boot* partition
- ○ There are *two* logical volumes in the vg_p2v01 volume group; they are vg_p2v01-lv_root and vg_p2v01-lv_swap
- ○ Here, vg_p2v01-lv_root is a root partition with the *ext4 filesystem*
- ○ vg_p2v01-lv_swap is a *swap partition*

3. Next, we need to prepare the boot information of our VM from the source machine. Extract the first 512 bytes, which is the **Master Boot Record** (**MBR**), into a file (source-mbr.bin) using the following command:

```
[root@source]# dd if=/dev/sda of=/backup/source-mbr.bin \
bs=512 count=1
```

We define the block size (bs) as 512 bytes and the write value as one (count=1).

4. Then, we need to extract the following information from the boot partition:

```
[root@source]# dd if=/dev/sda1 of=/backup/source-boot-part.img
bs=1M
```

5. If there is any LVM inside the source machine, we have to make a backup of its configuration with the vgcfgbackup command, as shown in the following command:

```
[root@source]# vgcfgbackup -f /backup/source-lvm.cfg
Volume group "vg_p2v01" successfully backed up.
```

6. Transfer the files from the source to vmsrv01:

```
[root@source]# scp /backup/* root@192.168.1.57:/backup
```

Next, we need to prepare the data source for our VM. Since we have used LVM in our source server, we would be able to create an LVM snapshot volume to prevent any change during our copy operation. If you don't have an LVM volume on your source server, you can simply skip the next part and move on to the *Preparing for migration on a Proxmox server* section.

Creating an LVM snapshot volume for data copying

Of course, this method is only available if you have used LVM volume on your source server. This is the preferred method because you don't need to stop the services in your physical machine as the changes are only applied on the snapshot. Please note the steps covered in the following points are executed in the source server.

An LVM snapshot requires around *15 percent to 20 percent disk space of the original volume*; make sure you have enough room to save the data.

1. Using the following command, we will check whether we have free physical extents for our LVM snapshot:

```
[root@source]# pvdisplay -m
PV Name               /dev/sda2
VG Name               vg_p2v01
Total PE              2434
Free PE               1280
```

As we can see, there are 1280 **physical extents** (PE) available for use.

 If you do not have a free PE for a snapshot, you can shrink down your LVM volume, but it requires a system shutdown. Please refer the *System migration of a Windows platform* section as your read more on offline migration ona physical machine with Linux platform to a KVM.

2. Next, we create our LVM volume with the `lvcreate` command and tell the system that it is a snapshot of the `lv_root` volume:

```
[root@source]# lvcreate -s -n mysnap -L800M /dev/vg_p2v01/lv_root
```

No error is returned because we only need 20% of original disk space (3.5GB * 0.2 = 702MB), so we have no problem creating a volume named mysnap with 800MB size.

3. We can create a directory as a mount point and mount the read-only volume `mysnap` to it using the following command:

```
[root@source]# mkdir /mnt/source
[root@source]# mount /dev/vg_p2v01/mysnap /mnt/source
```

4. If you have enabled SELinux, make sure that you have issued the following command to reset the security context (extended attributes added by SELinux):

```
[root@source]# restorecon -R -v /mnt/source
```

Then, we have to perform a restore with the backup files on the virtual machine. This includes the partition table recovery and LVM volume configuration restore.

Preparing for migration on a Proxmox server

After we have transferred the backup files to the Proxmox server, we have to create a blank KVM-based VM via a web GUI:

1. Choose the **Create VM** button from the top-right corner and fill in the following information:
    - **Node**: vmsrv01
    - **VM ID**: 302
    - **Name**: p2v-02

2. Since we are migrating to a Linux server, we choose **Linux 3.x/2.6 kernel** as the OS type.

3. We choose **Do not use any media option** in the **CD/DVD** tab as we are not performing installation from the disc.

4. Then, we need to build a virtual disk with a size that is identical to the source server:

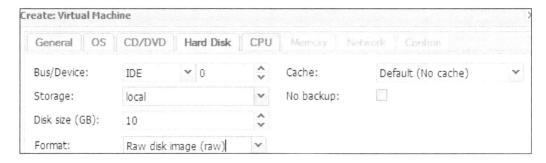

5. We have to set up two cores in the **CPU** tab, as shown in the following screenshot:

6. We have to identify the memory size, 1 GB, which is the same as that of the source, as shown in the following screenshot:

7. For the network part, simply accept the default setting.

8. Click on **Finish** to complete the process.

In the next part, we need to work in the command-line interface to restore disk information and copy data from the source server.

Restoring disk information from the source backup

Now, we have transferred the backup files that contain disk information, including the LVM structure information. It's time for us to restore them to the virtual disk for our new machine. The following steps will help you achieve that:

1. In the beginning, we have to restore the master boot record from the backup file /backup/source-mbr.bin using the following command:

```
[root@vmsrv01]# dd if=/backup/source-mbr.bin \
of=/var/lib/vz/images/302/vm-302-disk-1.raw \
conv=notrunc
```

2. Next, we need to install the kpartx package to mount our image using the following command:

```
[root@vmsrv01]# apt-get install kpartx
```

If you cannot install kpartx, you might need to update your Proxmox system first using the following command:

```
[root@vmsrv01]# aptitude update
```

 Kpartx is a command-line tool used to view the partitions for an image file. The partitions can be mounted at /dev/loop0 for the read/write process. Please refer to http://goo.gl/Io9VkP for more details.

3. Then, we can mount the KVM disk image to `/dev/loop0` using the following command:

```
[root@vmsrv01]# kpartx -av /var/lib/vz/images/302/vm-302-disk-1.
raw
```

4. To list the partitions inside the file, use the following command:

```
[root@vmsrv01]# fdisk -l /dev/loop0
Disk /dev/loop0: 10.7 GB, 10739318784 bytes
...
       Device Boot      Start         End      Blocks   Id  System
/dev/loop0p1    *           1          64      512000   83  Linux
/dev/loop0p2               64        1306     9972736   8e  Linux
LVM
```

This command will show the same partition layout as the source server.

5. After that, we need to restore the boot partition using the following command:

```
[root@vmsrv01]# dd if=/backup/source-boot-part.img \ of=/dev/
mapper/loop0p1 bs=1M
```

6. If you have an LVM volume, open the LVM configuration file `/backup/source-lvm.cfg` and find the ID under the `physical_volumes` section:

```
physical_volumes {
  pv0 {
    id = "RZ7PZh-RJlN-SZ09-Rw25-NZfo-H1Yn-cTidgs"
```

7. Before we can restore LVM settings, make sure your server does not contain PV with the same ID or the same name for the LVM volume using the `vgdisplay` and `pvscan` commands:

```
[root@vmsrv01]# pvscan
[root@vmsrv01]# vgdisplay | grep "PV Name"
```

If you already have an LVM volume with the same name, you might need to rename your existing volume to another name using the `vgrename` command. Please refer to `http://linux.die.net/man/8/vgrename` for more information on the `vgrename` command.

8. Restore the LVM configuration using the `pvcreate` and `vgcfgrestore` commands:

```
[root@vmsrv01]# pvcreate -u RZ7PZh-RJlN-SZ09-Rw25-NZfo-H1Yn-cTidgs
\
--restore /backup/source-lvm.cfg /dev/mapper/loop0p2

[root@vmsrv01]# vgcfgrestore -f /backup/source-lvm.cfg vg_p2v01
  Restored volume group vg_p2v01
```

9. When everything is done, check the LVM information with the pvs, vgs, and lvs commands:

```
[root@vmsrv01]# pvs
PV                          VG              Fmt Attr PSize PFree
/dev/mapper/loop0p2         vg_p2v01        lvm2 a-- 9.51g 5.00g

[root@vmsrv01]# vgs
VG       #PV #LV #SN Attr   VSize   VFree
vg_p2v01 1   2   0 wz--n-   9.51g   5.00g

[root@vmsrv01]# lvs
LV           VG            Attr       LSize Pool Origin Data%
lv_root      vg_p2v01      -wi------ 3.51g
lv_swap      vg_p2v01      -wi------ 1.00g
```

10. Next, we need to create the filesystem(s) for the LVM image file; lv_swap is a swap partition and lv_root is the root partition with the ext4 filesystem:

```
[root@vmsrv01]# vgchange -ay vg_p2v01
[root@vmsrv01]# mkswap /dev/vg_p2v01/lv_swap
[root@vmsrv01]# mkfs.ext4 /dev/vg_p2v01/lv_root
```

11. Create a directory as the mount point and mount lv_root to it using the following command:

```
[root@vmsrv01]# mkdir /mnt/source
[root@vmsrv01]# mount /dev/vg_p2v01/lv_root /mnt/source
```

Up to this point, we have built a partition layout on our VM that is identical to that of the source machine. In the next step, we need to copy data from the source.

Copying data from the source server to the Proxmox server

In the previous section, we mounted our data volume to /mnt/source as the data source for the Proxmox server. The following are the steps to copy data from the source machine to the destination machine:

1. Start our copy operation by issuing the rsync command; it will take a couple of minutes to complete the command:

```
[root@source]# rsync -avz -H  -A -X /mnt/source \
root@192.168.1.57:/mnt/source
```

If you haven't mounted the LVM snapshot volume from the previous section, you need to create an exclude directory list first, as shown in the following lines of code:

```
/tmp/exclude.txt:
/tmp
/lost+found
/mnt
/proc
/tmp
/sys
```

2. Assume that we have mounted a partition by mapping our virtual disk image file with the `kpartx` command to `/mnt/source` in the Proxmox server; issue the following command to start the copy operation:

```
[root@source]# rsync -auz -H -X / --exclude--from=/tmp/exclude.txt
root@192.168.1.57:/mnt/source
```

3. As the LVM snapshot will not include mount points, there are a few directories that need to be copied manually:

```
[root@source]# rsync -auz -H -X /boot \
root@192.168.1.57:/mnt/source/boot
[root@source]# rsync -auz -H -X /selinux \
root@192.168.1.57:/mnt/source/boot
[root@source]# rsync -auz -H -X /dev \
root@192.168.1.57:/mnt/source/dev
```

4. If you have custom mount points (for example, `/download`) and an additional hard disk with the `ext4` filesystem (for example, `/dev/sdb1`) in your physical machine, you might need to do the following (this is optional):

   ○ Add an extra virtual hard drive first and create a mount point in the VM using the following command:

   ```
   [root@vmsrv01]# mkdir /mnt/source/download
   ```

   ○ Simply copy the data from the mount point first using the following command:

   ```
   [root@vmsrv01]# rsync -avz -H -X /download \
   root@192.168.1.57:/mnt/source/download
   ```

   ○ Edit the `/etc/fstab` file to reflect the mount point:

   ```
   /dev/sdb1 /download ext4 defaults 0 0
   ```

5. We can list out the content under `/mnt/source` in Proxmox after the copy operation is finished using the following command:

   ```
   [root@vmsrv01]# ls /mnt/source
   ```

6. Before booting up our VM, we have to change the IP address for the VM to a temporary one, for example, `192.168.1.39`. Also, the default Ethernet adapter (`eth0`) is unlikely to be used because the network card is different from the source server's network card. So, the network card in the VM will be bonded with `eth1` instead. We need to copy the original configuration file to form a new one. Then, change the IP address for this network card for testing purposes:

```
[root@vmsrv01]# cd /mnt/source/etc/sysconfig/network-scripts/
[root@vmsrv01 network-scripts]# cp ifcfg-eth0 ifcfg-eth1
[root@vmsrv01 network-scripts]# nano ifcfg-eth1
```

7. Change the IP address and remove the HWADDR option if it is defined:

```
Change: IPADDR=192.168.1.32 to IPADDR=192.168.1.39
Remove this: HWADDR=02:33:DC:EA:92:FE
```

8. We can dismount the virtual disk image from our Proxmox server using the following commands:

```
[root@vmsrv01]# umount /mnt/source
[root@vmsrv01]# vgchange -an vg_p2v01
[root@vmsrv01]# kpartx -dv \
/var/lib/vz/images/302/vm-302-disk-1.raw
```

9. Then, start the VM via the web console.

10. Test whether the server is back online using the `ping` command:

```
[root@vmsrv01]# ping 192.168.1.39
```

11. If everything works fine, shut down the physical machine and change the IP address of the VM back to `192.168.1.32`.

12. We can further reduce the allocated size for the virtual disk by converting it to the qcow2 format (optional). Please note that this is *not* an essential process:

```
[root@vmsrv01]# qemu-img convert -O qcow2 \
/var/lib/vz/images/302/vm-302-disk-1.raw \
/var/lib/vz/images/302/vm-302-disk-1.qcow2
```

13. You can see that there is a significant difference in size between the two files because only used data space will be preserved in the qcow2 file format:

```
2388000768 vm-302-disk-1.qcow2
10737418240 vm-302-disk-1.raw
```

14. Edit the VM configuration file at `/etc/pve/qemu-server/302.conf` as follows:

```
From: ide0: local:302/vm-302-disk-1.raw,size=10G
To: ide0: local:302/vm-302-disk-1.qcow2,size=10G
```

15. Remove the raw file to save disk space:

```
[root@vmsrv01]# rm /var/lib/vz/images/302/vm-302-disk1.raw
```

System migration of a Windows platform

If turning off the physical machine is possible, then this process is much easier. The main concept is to use a live CD to boot up the system and then copy the source data to the target VM. Since this method makes a full clone of the source system, it is suitable for both the Linux and Windows platforms.

If you are planning to move a domain controller that is running with Active Directory, then this method is *not* going to work because you cannot simply clone the operating system. Simple instructions on this are listed at http://goo.gl/Z5jO7j; for more details, you can refer to articles from Microsoft at http://goo.gl/yx0BPG.

The following steps will guide you through the migration of a Windows platform:

1. The first thing we need to do is build a blank KVM machine with VM ID *303*, which will be running on a Linux platform, and VM ID *304*, which will be running on a Windows platform, and name them as p2v-03 and p2v-04; please refer to the configuration steps covered in *Chapter 4, Configuring a Proxmox VE Cluster*, on how to create VM 302.

2. Then, we need to perform the following procedure to clone an existing system. We need to make use of a Clonezilla live CD for the operation; download the ISO file at (normally choosing i686 should be enough) http://goo.gl/hvZHgM.

3. Burn the ISO file on a CD-ROM and prepare to turn off the source machine.

4. Insert the CD with Clonezilla and choose *Clonezilla live* as shown in the following screenshot:

```
          clonezilla.org, clonezilla.nchc.org.tw

Clonezilla live (Default settings, VGA 800x600)
```

5. Choose **Don't touch keymap** to use the default keyboard layout, as shown in the following screenshot:

```
Policy for handling keymaps:

                Select keymap from arch list
                Don't touch keymap
```

6. To enable the command-line interface, choose **Enter Shell** first, as shown in the following screenshot:

```
Start Clonezilla or enter login shell (command line)?
Select mode:

        Start_Clonezilla Start Clonezilla
        Enter_shell      Enter command line prompt
```

7. Then, choose **cmd** in the next screen, as shown in the following screenshot:

```
Now you can choose to:

poweroff Poweroff
reboot   Reboot
cmd      Enter command line prompt
```

8. Now, we can assign a temporary IP address on the source server using the following commands:

```
[user@debian]$ sudo su
[root@debian]# ifconfig eth0 192.168.1.32 netmask 255.255.255.0 up
```

You can even assign an IP address with DHCP if you have a local DHCP server, as shown in the following command:

```
[user@debian]$ sudo su
[root@debian]# dhclient eth0
```

9. Then, we can copy the data to the virtual disk image file located in our Proxmox server:

```
[root@debian]# dd if=/dev/sda | ssh root@192.168.1.57 \
dd of=/var/lib/vz/images/303/vm-303-disk-1.raw
```

10. To save disk space, we will convert the disk image to the qcow2 format in our Proxmox server using the following command (optional):

```
[root@vmsrv01]# qemu-img convert -O qcow2 \
/var/lib/vz/images/303/vm-303-disk-1.raw \
/var/lib/vz/images/303/vm-303-disk-1.qcow2
```

11. Change the `ide0` value in the VM configuration file to use the new disk image:

```
[root@vmsrv01]# nano /etc/pve/qemu-server/303.conf
ide0: local:303/vm-303-disk-1.qcow2,size=10G
```

When we migrate a Windows platform to VM ID 304, you need to perform the same steps that we just covered. You will just need to change all the *303* keywords to *304* and change the IP address to *192.168.1.34* instead. So, we have prepared our VM with a copy of data from the source server. Let's check out the post-migration tasks we need to perform.

Post-migration for offline migration with a physical machine

For a Linux system, everything should run fine with block-level data copying, as mentioned previously. We only need to fix the network interface configuration problem that has been listed in the online migration section in the following location:

```
[root@p2v-03]# cp /etc/sysconfig/network-scripts/ifcfg-eth0 \
/etc/sysconfig/network-scripts/ifcfg-eth1

[root@p2v-03]# nano /etc/sysconfig/network-scripts/ifcfg-eth1
```

For the Windows platform (VM 304), we are likely to run into a **blue screen of death** (**BSOD**) because the system drivers do not match with the source machine and the virtualized machine. The entire process of migration has been explained in the following steps:

1. If you have encountered the following error when you boot up your VM after migration, you have to perform post-migration operations:

Your PC ran into a problem and needs to restart. We're just collecting some error info, and then we'll restart for you. (20% complete)

If you'd like to know more, you can search online later for this error: SYSTEM_THREAD_EXCEPTION_NOT_HANDLED (winhv.sys)

2. When you cannot boot up your system, you will be able to enter the *Auto Recovery* mode, as shown in the following screenshot. You should choose **Troubleshoot** in this screen:

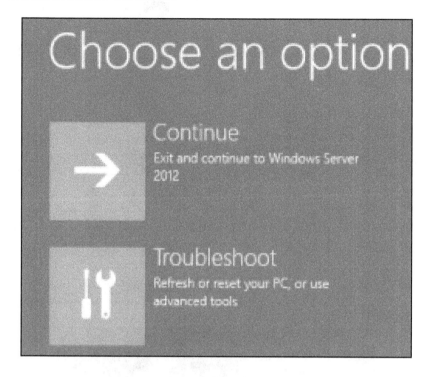

3. Within the three options, we choose **Startup Settings**:

4. Next, the system will boot up with a *traditional boot menu* (for example, the boot menu you get when you press *F8* in the previous version of Windows):

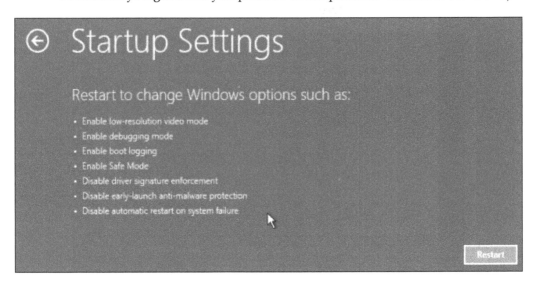

5. We choose **Safe Mode** in order to avoid additional drivers being loaded, which may cause the system to crash, as shown in the following screenshot:

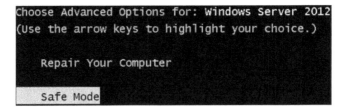

6. Now, we should be able to enter the system in safe mode. Then, we open the *Device Manager* and search to see whether there is a device shown with errors. If we find one, we have to remove it, as shown in the following screenshot:

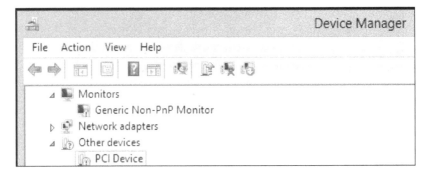

7. When finished, reboot the system to see if everything is working.

In this section, we have successfully moved our existing system from a physical server to a VM. Next, we are going to introduce the process of converting VMs from different virtual appliances to a Proxmox server.

System migration from VMware to Proxmox

If you want to move a VMware-based VM to an OpenVZ container, please refer to the *Live migration of a physical machine to a KVM* section. Note that it only works for Linux platforms.

To migrate a system to a KVM-based VM, you can use Clonezilla to copy the system content by referring to the *System migration of a Windows platform* section. Just remember that you have to remove VMware Tools if you have already installed them on the source VM.

Rather than cloning the content, we can simply import the virtual disk of the source VM because Proxmox supports the VMware format. Please note that the following applies to a Linux environment too; you just need to skip the Windows-specific options.

To enhance the performance, you will likely need to install VMware Tools for your existing system. If you want to have a smooth migration, it is essential to *remove VMware Tools* from the existing system. You can refer to `http://goo.gl/kyheH6` for more information on this. The following steps will guide you through the process of making native IDE driver for our source platform in order to reduce the chance of getting boot up problems:

1. First, start the VM from a Windows platform and download the `Mergeide.zip` file from `http://goo.gl/Ju5t00`.

2. When the file download is finished, extract it and execute `mergeide.reg` to change the Windows registry to *allow Windows to boot from IDE* (Windows only).

3. Check whether `Atapi.sys`, `Intelide.sys`, `Pciide.sys`, and `Pciidex.sys` are in the `%SystemRoot%\System32\Drivers` folder (Windows only). If there is any missing file, copy the files back from `%SystemRoot%\Driver Cache\I386\Driver.cab`.

4. Now, make sure that the virtual disk that was used by VMware is a single file; that is, there is only one file with the vmdk extension in the VM storage. If the virtual disk is split into multiple files as shown in the following screenshot (with extensions s001.vmdk, s002.vmdk, and so on), we need to use the vmware-vdiskmanager command to combine them into a single file:

Windows Server 2012.vmdk	4/6/2014 15:15	VMDK File	2 KB
Windows Server 2012-s001.vmdk	5/6/2014 18:04	VMDK File	1,437,888 KB
Windows Server 2012-s002.vmdk	5/6/2014 18:04	VMDK File	1,928,640 KB
Windows Server 2012-s003.vmdk	5/6/2014 18:04	VMDK File	2,077,824 KB
Windows Server 2012-s004.vmdk	5/6/2014 18:04	VMDK File	2,072,128 KB
Windows Server 2012-s005.vmdk	5/6/2014 18:04	VMDK File	870,016 KB
Windows Server 2012-s006.vmdk	5/6/2014 18:04	VMDK File	30,592 KB

The reason for splitting a large single file in to smaller fixed-sized files is that there might be a single maximum file size limit in some operation systems. Also, it is much easier for us to move smaller files than to move a file with a huge size. Therefore, it is the default option selected when you create a VM under the VMware platform.

Since the vmware-vdiskmanager command is not available in both the VMware player and vSphere client, we have to download *vSphere 5.0.3 Virtual Disk Development Kit* via the link http://goo.gl/tzJ03s; you will require a VMware account to download it. You can choose either a Windows or Linux version based on the operating system in your workstation. The following steps will guide us in migrating our existing operating system from a VMware-based environment to Proxmox:

1. Turn off your Windows VM and copy your virtual disk files including Win2012-s001.vmdk, Win2012-s002.vmdk, and so on to where you have vSphere 5.0.3 Virtual Disk Development Kit installed.

2. For a Windows version, open the command prompt and enter the following command to start the conversion. For example, my virtual disk is located at D:\VM, so I will issue the following command:

```
c:\program files (x86)\VMware\VMware Virtual Disk Development Kit\
bin\vmware-vdiskmanager.exe -r D:\VM\Win2012.vmdk -t 0 D:\WM\
Win2012_merged.vmdk
```

```
-r: refers to source disk name    -t 0: means to create a single
file
```

3. For Linux, extract the `gzip` file and place the virtual disk image file in `/root`. Then, execute the following command. `[32|64]` refers to a 32- or 64-bit platform:

```
[root@local:/root]# ./vmware-vix-disklib-distrib/bin[32|64]/
vmware-vdiskmanager -r Win2012.vmdk -t 0 Win2012_merged.vmdk
```

4. Create a new blank KVM-based VM with VM ID 305. Copy the newly created virtual disk file to the directory (`/var/lib/vz/images/305`) in Proxmox using FileZilla (if you are using Windows) with the following login information via the SSH tunnel:

   ○ **Host**: `192.168.1.57`

   ○ **User**: `root`

   ○ **Password**: `<your_password_for_Proxmox>`

   ○ **Port**: `22`

   If you are using Linux, you can transfer the image file with the following command:

```
[root@local:/root]# scp Win2012_merged.vmdk \
root@192.168.1.57:/var/lib/vz/images/305
```

5. Tell the VM to use the new image by modifying the configuration file at `/etc/pve/qemu-server/305.conf`:

```
ide0: local:305/Win2012_merged.vmdk,format=vmdk,size=20G
```

6. Boot up the system and configure the network settings and other settings. If you find a BSOD problem, solve it by referring to the *Post-migration for offline migration with a physical machine* section.

In the next section, we will see how we can migrate from XenServer.

System migration from XenServer / Hyper-V Server to Proxmox

Although these two virtualization platforms (XenServer / Hyper-V Server) are different, they can both export VMs into a VHD file.

When we deal with the Xen environment, we can make use of the methods mentioned in the *Live migration of a physical machine to a KVM* section. However, I would also like to provide another method by exporting a VM from XenServer and then importing it back to the Proxmox environment.

If you have a Hyper-V environment, you can directly start from step 6 to skip the XenServer-related steps. The concept here is to turn off the VM and find out the storage location, copy the VHD file to Proxmox, and execute the disk image conversion command.

The steps involved in system migration for both XenServer and Hyper-V Server are as follows:

1. Before starting the migration, it is recommended to remove *XenServer Tools* to avoid any system driver conflicts.

2. We can export a VM from XenServer using XenCenter, a management tool for VM management, or using the XenServer command line. If we choose to use XenCenter, choose the VM you would like to export, as shown in the following screenshot:

3. Before we can start the export process, we need to *turn off the source VM*. Then, choose the VM from the top menu and choose **Export...**.

4. A wizard will open, and we need to specify the export **Location**. Here, I define the location path as D:\VM:

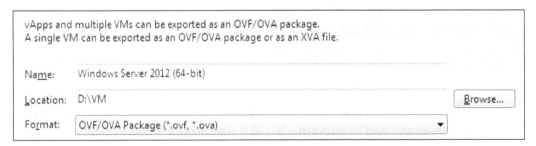

5. We need to select the VM for export. Since we already selected this in step 1, the VM is automatically selected; now, follow these steps:

   ○ Don't specify the EULA for use.

   ○ Don't specify **Advanced Options** and choose **Next**.

   ○ Assign a temporary IP address, `192.168.1.39`, to the VM.

   ○ Click on **Finish** to start the export operation.

6. When the export operation is completed, there will be two output files—one **VHD (Virtual Hard Disk)** file named with a random string and one **OVF (Open Virtualization Format)** file. VHD is a file that contains the system content, and OVF can be treated as the configuration file for this VM. For more information, check out the following links:

   ○ VHD: `http://en.wikipedia.org/wiki/VHD_%28file_format%29`

   ○ OVF: `http://en.wikipedia.org/wiki/Open_Virtualization_Format`

7. Create a new VM with ID 306, and make sure that you have configured it with the same number of CPUs and memory.

8. Transfer the VHD file to Proxmox at `/var/lib/vz/images/306`.

9. Then, issue the following command to convert the VHD file to a Proxmox-supported file format, for example, `qcow2`. Assume that we have a VHD file named `29de62e1-11dd-4d6f-9c80-6bccf020db1d.vhd` stored in the directory `/var/lib/vz/images/306`:

   ```
   [root@vmsrv01]# qemu-img convert -f vpc -O qcow2 \
   /var/lib/vz/images/306/29de62e1-11dd-4d6f-9c80-6bccf020db1d.vhd \
   /var/lib/vz/images/306/vm-306-disk-1.qcow2
   ```

10. Set up the configuration file for VM 306 at `/etc/pve/qemu-server/306.conf` with the following code:

    ```
    ide0: local:306/vm-306-disk-1.qcow2,size=20G
    ```

11. Start VM 306 to see if there is any problem.

In this section, I have demonstrated how to perform system migration of a VM from XenServer and Hyper-V Server to Proxmox.

Summary

In this chapter, we have gone through the system migration processes for different scenarios including a physical machine, VMware, XenServer, and Hyper-V Server to either OpenVZ containers or KVM-based VMs. In most cases, suffering from downtime is inevitable, which means that we have to make a proper plan before starting with the migration.

Next, we will take a look at how to perform the backup/restore processes on the Proxmox server, create an OpenVZ template for future deployment, and recover a failed Proxmox cluster.

7
Disaster Recovery on a Proxmox VE Cluster

In the previous chapters, we covered different concepts of virtualization methods and the components needed for a cluster environment. We learned how to build shared storages with DRBD, GlusterFS, CEPH, and others, and how to implement them under Proxmox to build an HA environment. We also learned how to move our existing operating systems to Proxmox.

You might notice that you are centralizing your production platforms in one server. From a system administrator's perspective, if we do not have any backup in hand, it is very dangerous. Therefore, we will go through the backup and restore processes of Proxmox in this chapter, including the following topics:

- Backup and restore processes of OpenVZ containers and KVM
- Creating a system template for OpenVZ for further use
- Backup and restore processes for a Proxmox cluster
- Recovering from a failed Proxmox cluster

Let's find out how we can make our own backup for the VMs. Note that during the backup process, you might lose your existing backup files. Make sure you have stored your existing backup to another location before you start the following tutorials.

Backup process for VMs in Proxmox

From the previous chapters, we know that a VM is controlled by two different components: the configuration file and the data inside the VM (the virtual disk in a KVM and the workspace in an OpenVZ environment). In the upcoming sections, we will go through the process of backing up these two components.

Backing up the configuration files of a Proxmox cluster

In *Chapter 2*, *Getting Started with a High Availability (HA) Environment*, we mentioned where the configuration files are located.

- For OpenVZ, the files are located at /etc/pve/nodes/${Proxmox_hostname}/ openvz

- For KVM, the files are located at /etc/pve/nodes/${Proxmox_hostname}/ qemu-server

As the configuration files are only stored in plain text format, we can simply pack them up with the TAR command. For example, we issue the following commands under the Proxmox server (vmsrv01) and change their directory to /etc/pve/ nodes/vmsrv01:

```
root@vmsrv01:/etc/pve/nodes/vmsrv01# tar -czf openvz-backup.tgz openvz
root@vmsrv01:/etc/pve/nodes/vmsrv01# tar -czf kvm-backup.tgz qemu-server
root@vmsrv01:/etc/pve/nodes/vmsrv01# mv openvz-backup.tgz /backup/
root@vmsrv01:/etc/pve/nodes/vmsrv01# mv kvm-backup.tgz /backup
```

In these commands, we created a copy of all the configuration files at /backup for both the OpenVZ containers and the KVM VMs as tar files named openvz-backup and kvm-backup, respectively, with gzip enabled.

During the backup operation, the associated OpenVZ/KVM configuration is automatically backed up using the vzdump command, which will be introduced in the next section.

Therefore, if you have backed up all of your VMs with the vzdump command or via the web GUI, you can skip this part or create a separate configuration backup for safety reasons.

Now, we have to create a backup copy of the following configuration files:

- `/etc/pve/cluster.conf`: This file stores the cluster information
- `/etv/pve/storage.cfg`: This file stores the available storage inside the cluster
- `/etc/pve/ceph.cfg`: This file stores the information of the CEPH server

We also have to copy the configuration files to `/backup` as our primary backup location using the following commands:

```
root@vmsrv01# cp /etc/pve/ceph.cfg /backup
root@vmsrv01# cp /etc/pve/cluster.conf /backup
root@vmsrv01# cp /etc/pve/storage.cfg /backup
```

Backing up the VM data in Proxmox

After we have made a copy of the container configuration files, we are going to back up the actual data inside the VM. There are two different methods to do this: manual backup using the `vzdump` command for both KVM and OpenVZ guests or backup via the GUI management console.

In our example, VM 100 will be used to demonstrate the OpenVZ container backup, while VM 101 will be used to demonstrate the KVM machine backup.

Backing up using the vzdump command for VMs

There are the following three different backup approaches when using the `vzdump` command:

- **Stop mode**: This stops the VM that takes a long time during backup.
- **Suspend mode**: This uses the `rsync` command to copy data to a temporary location (defined in `--tmpdir`) and then performs a second `rsync` operation while suspending the container. When the second `rsync` operation completes, the suspended VM is resumed.
- **Snapshot mode**: This mode makes use of the LVM2 snapshot function. It requires extra space within the LVM volume.

These operation modes are very similar to what we covered in *Chapter 6, System Migration of an Existing System to a Proxmox VE Cluster*. We will now go through all the possible methods one by one. Unless explicitly specified, the following sections are relevant to both the OpenVZ container and KVM VMs.

Backing up using the vzdump stop mode for the OpenVZ container

This is the simplest method to create a system backup if a certain amount of system downtime is acceptable. We need to stop the container first, dump the container data as an image file, and start the VM again. So, what is the advantage of using the vzdump command over the rsync command? If you are familiar with the OpenVZ container structure and feel confident to back up yourselves, then vzdump will have no advantage for you in the stop mode. However, if you are doubtful that you might lose files during your manual backup, then vzdump is a better solution for you, as it can pack all the necessary files to run the VMs.

In OpenVZ, vzctl is a command-line tool to manage any operation related to the OpenVZ container, including checking the status, starting/stopping the container, and even accessing the system itself. As we are required to turn off the container before taking a backup, the system downtime is a huge disadvantage of this method. Make sure that we don't have services running in the container. Log in with the root user account and follow these steps:

1. Use the following command to check the status of a container, for example, in VM 100:

   ```
   root@vmsrv01# vzlist 100
   CTID        NPROC STATUS    IP_ADDR         HOSTNAME
   100         4 running       192.168.1.10    myvm1.localdomain
   ```

   You can further check the process status of the container using the vztop and vzps commands that are equivalent to the top and ps commands of a Linux environment:

   ```
   root@vmsrv01# vztop -E 100
   ```

   ```
   root@vmsrv01# vzps -E 100
   ```

2. Now, we would like to turn the container off; we can do so with the vzctl command:

   ```
   root@vmsrv01# vzctl stop 100
   Stopping container ...
   Container was stopped
   Container is unmounted
   ```

3. Make sure the container is properly turned off:

   ```
   root@vmsrv01# vzlist 100
   CTID        NPROC STATUS    IP_ADDR         HOSTNAME
   100         -     stopped   -               myvm1.localdomain
   ```

4. Of course, you can also turn off the virtual machine with the `shutdown` command if your guest OS is running under Linux:

   ```
   root@vm01# shutdown -h now
   ```

5. Perform a backup process by issuing the following command:

   ```
   root@vmsrv01# vzdump 100
   ```

6. You might receive an error message, as shown in the following output:

   ```
   Can't use storage for backups - wrong content type
   ```

   This output means that the backup storage is not defined under Proxmox. Here, we can make use of the `local` keyword or create a new one with the web management console.

Defining a new backup storage location

To create a new backup storage location, we need to access the web management console with the help of the following steps:

1. Log in to the web interface, click on **Datacenter** on the left-hand side panel, and choose **Storage** from the right-hand side panel.

2. Create a new directory for the backup storage, if it does not exist, using the following command:

   ```
   root@vmsrv01# mkdir /backup
   ```

3. Click on **Add** from the right-hand side panel and choose **Directory** to open the **Add: Directory** window. Enter the information, as shown in the following screenshot. Make sure that the **Content** field is changed to **Backups**.

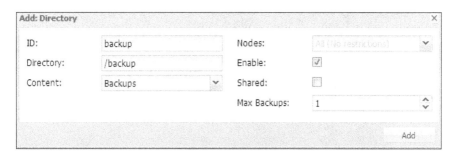

Now, we are back at creating the backup process for the OpenVZ container.

4. You should be able to perform the backup using our new storage location with the following command:

```
root@vmsrv01# vzdump 100 -storage backup
```

The keyword `backup` refers to the storage ID defined in the previous window, and the backup file will be placed in a directory named `dump` under the `/backup` directory. The following is the dump process log for VM 100:

```
INFO: Starting Backup of VM 100 (openvz)
INFO: CTID 100 exist unmounted down
. . .
INFO: creating archive '/backup/dump/vzdump-
openvz-100-2014_07_04-16_12_05.tar'
. . .
INFO: Finished Backup of VM 100 (00:00:41)
INFO: Backup job finished successfully
```

As we do not specify the backup mode, the *stop mode* is chosen, and the data is packed in a *TAR package for the OpenVZ container* by default. Moreover, `stdexcludes` is set to `1` by default; this means that the following files are excluded from the packages:

- `/var/log/.*`
- `/tmp/.*`
- `/var/tmp/.*`
- `/var/run/.*pid`

5. We can check out the result in the `/backup/dump` directory using the following command:

```
root@vmsrv01# ls -lh /backup/dump
-rw-r--r-- 1 root root 850M Jul  4 17:07 /backup/dump/vzdump-
openvz-100-2014_07_04-17_06_52.tar
```

The file is named in the following format:

```
vzdump-openvz-<VMID>-YYYY_MM_DD-HH_MM_SS.tar
```

 Make sure that your backup file follows the naming format and is not changed, as the GUI expects this format.

6. The backup was finished successfully, but we found that it requires a lot of space as the data is not compressed. To enable compression, use the `-compress` option with `vzdump`:

```
root@vmsrv01# vzdump 100 -storage backup -compress gzip
```

7. Again, we can check the size difference between the `tar` package and GZIP package using the following command:

```
root@vmsrv01# ls -lh /backup/dump
-rw-r--r-- 1 root root 850M Jul  4 17:07 /backup/dump/vzdump-
openvz-100-2014_07_04-17_06_52.tar
-rw-r--r-- 1 root root 338M Jul  4 17:22 /backup/dump/vzdump-
openvz-100-2014_07_04-17_21_13.tar.gz
```

There is an obvious difference in size between the two files. Therefore, I recommended that you compress the backup file to save space. We don't need to back up the configuration file manually because the VM configuration file will be copied to `/etc/vzdump/vps.conf`.

Backing up with vzdump stop mode for KVM

Backing up with KVM is similar to the backup process of an OpenVZ container, but there are a few differences during the backup stage. Here are the steps to backup a KVM:

1. Make sure that your VM is properly turned off.

2. Issue the `vzdump` command as follows:

```
root@vmsrv01# vzdump 101 -storage backup
INFO: Starting Backup of VM 101 (qemu)
...
INFO: starting kvm to execute backup task
INFO: creating archive '/backup/dump/vzdump-
qemu-101-2014_07_05-23_36_29.vma'
...
INFO: status: 0% (34340864/8589934592), sparse 0% (12648448),
duration 3, 11/7 MB/s
...
INFO: status: 100% (8589934592/8589934592), sparse 84%
(7282487296), duration 189, 212/2 MB/s
INFO: stopping kvm after backup task
INFO: Finished Backup of VM 101 (00:03:12)
INFO: Backup job finished successfully
```

3. For an OpenVZ-based VM, the VM remains suspended during the backup operation, but the KVM will be *turned on* during the backup process, as shown in the following screenshot:

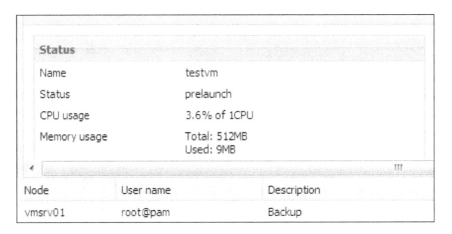

 The file is named using the following format:

```
vzdump-qemu-<VMID>-YYYY_MM_DD-HH_MM_SS.vma
```

Starting from Proxmox Version 2.3, a new file format, VMA, was introduced to replace the old common TAR format as the default output file option for KVM-based machines.

The VMA file format was developed by Proxmox in order to use just one format for the backup file, and it deals with the overheads that the snapshot might have generated. Besides, this file format can work with any storage type and image format, and *no temporary storage is required during backup*. Moreover, the most important point is that *only used blocks will be copied* to the backup file; this slightly reduces the size of the output file. For more details, please refer to http://pve.proxmox.com/wiki/VMA.

4. We can check out the result in the /backup/dump directory using the following command:

```
root@vmsrv01# ls -lh /backup/dump
-rw-r--r-- 1 root root 1.3G Jul  4 23:39 vzdump-
qemu-101-2014_07_05-23_36_29.vma
```

5. We can further reduce the output file's size by enabling compression; this can be done with the following command:

```
root@vmsrv01# vzdump 101 -storage backup -compress gzip
```

6. We can check out the result files in the `/backup/dump` directory:

```
-rw-r--r-- 1 root root 1.3G Jul  4 23:39
vzdump-qemu-101-2014_07_05-23_36_29.vma
-rw-r--r-- 1 root root 445M Jul  5 23:58 vzdump-
qemu-101-2014_07_05-23_55_25.vma.gz
```

Backing up with the vzdump suspend mode

Although the preceding method is simple, it has already taken around 1 minute to completely back up a 900 MB container. How about if we have a container that is several gigabytes in size? It was observed that the backup duration is slightly more if the data size of the container is increased; this results in a longer system downtime. So, let's try something else: `vzdump suspend` mode.

Before we start, make sure you have enough disk space and have defined a backup storage location for this demonstration. In the following example, the backup storage `/backup` is used as created in the preceding command:

1. To start with, turn on the VM.

2. Then, we can issue the `vzdump` command for backup testing:

```
root@vmsrv01# vzdump 100 -storage backup -compress gzip -mode
suspend
...
INFO: status = running
INFO: backup mode: suspend
INFO: starting first sync /var/lib/vz/private/100/ to /backup/
dump/vzdump-openvz-100-2014_07_04-18_01_46.tmp
...
INFO: first sync finished (15 seconds)
INFO: suspend vm
INFO: Setting up checkpoint...
...
INFO: starting final sync /var/lib/vz/private/100/ to /backup/
dump/vzdump-openvz-100-2014_07_04-18_01_46.tmp
INFO: final sync finished (0 seconds)
INFO: Resuming...
INFO: vm is online again after 3 seconds
INFO: creating archive '/backup/dump/vzdump-
openvz-100-2014_07_05-16_44_41.tar.gz'
...
INFO: Finished Backup of VM 100 (00:02:34)
INFO: Backup job finished successfully
```

3. During a backup operation, we will suffer from a short period of no-response time, *depending on the size of our container*. In my example, I am backing up a system that is less than 1 GB in size; here is my response time result:

```
64 bytes from 192.168.1.10: icmp_req=83 ttl=63 time=0.249 ms
64 bytes from 192.168.1.10: icmp_req=84 ttl=63 time=1.32 ms
64 bytes from 192.168.1.10: icmp_req=85 ttl=63 time=0.272 ms
```

4. We can check out the output file at /backup/dump again:

```
root@vmsrv01# ls -lh /backup/dump
-rw-r--r-- 1 root root 338M Jul  4 17:22 /backup/dump/vzdump-
openvz-100-2014_07_04-17_21_13.tar.gz
```

As you can see, the system downtime is set to minimum, but it is not guaranteed. With the use of an LVM snapshot, we will enjoy the ability to back up a running system without the need to make the services unavailable.

Preparation for using the LVM snapshot with vzdump

Backing up with an LVM snapshot is the best solution among the methods described earlier as we can have guaranteed zero system downtime, but it requires some preparation first. Before we can move on, let's check the following criteria:

- You need *at least 512 MB* free space in your LVM volume group, which means that you need to have *free physical extents* in your VG volume. You can check the memory usage with the help of the following command:

```
root@vmsrv01:~# vgdisplay
--- Volume group ---
VG Name                pve
Total PE               28490
Alloc PE / Size        24939 / 97.42 GiB
Free  PE / Size        3551 / 13.87 GiB
```

 In this example, we have 13.87 GB free space that can be used to create an LVM snapshot.

- You cannot place your backup in the same LVM volume that contains VM data. By default, your VM is in /pve/data, which is mounted as /var/lib/vz. You cannot back up the data in the same LVM volume at /var/lib/vz/dump. In this case, you have to define a new backup location for the LVM snapshot to take place. If you don't have a separate LVM volume under the existing system, you might need to create a new LVM volume. This is described in the following section.

Creating a new LVM volume for backup storage

Assume that you have a new physical storage available at /dev/sdd1. Then, using the following steps, you can create a separate LVM volume as the backup storage:

1. Create the base physical volume with the pvcreate command:

    ```
    root@vmsrv01# pvcreate /dev/sdd1
    ```

2. Create a new volume group (for example, backup-store) with the vgcreate command:

    ```
    root@vmsrv01# vgcreate backup-store /dev/sdd1
    ```

3. Create a new logical volume with a size of 10 GB, for example, for the filesystem with the lvcreate command:

    ```
    root@vmsrv01# lvcreate -L10G --name backup-data backup-store
    ```

4. If you want to use all the space that is available in the volume group, check the number of free extents with the vgdisplay command first:

    ```
    root@vmsrv01# vgdisplay backup-store
    Free  PE / Size        3551 / 13.87 GiB
    ```

    Then, we can assign the new logical volume with all the free extents available using the following command:

    ```
    root@vmsrv01# lvcreate -L 3551 --name backup-data backup-store
    ```

5. Format the logical volume with the filesystem for system use:

    ```
    root@vmsrv01# mkfs.ext4 /dev/backup-store/backup-data
    ```

6. Create a new directory that is to be used as the system mount point:

    ```
    root@vmsrv01# mkdir /mybackup
    ```

7. Mount the filesystem for usage:

    ```
    root@vmsrv01# mount /dev/backup-store/backup-data /mybackup
    ```

8. Then, follow the instructions from the previous section, *Defining a new backup storage location.*

If you do not have enough free physical extents but you have not used up all the space, you can either resize the existing LV to free up space or add additional physical devices to the VG to increase the usable space.

Reducing the size of an LVM's logical volume

Assume that we have an LVM volume group (`mygroup`) and a logical volume (`backup`) of 20 GB disk size, formatted with `ext4` and mounted at `/backup`. Let's check out the steps to resize the logical volume to 10 GB to free up some space:

1. To check the current disk usage of the logical volume, we can use the following command:

   ```
   root@vmsrv01# lvdisplay
   ```

   ```
   LV Path              /dev/mygroup/backup
   LV Name              backup
   VG Name              mygroup
   LV Size              20.0 GiB
   ```

2. Then, we have to dismount the volume before we can actually shrink it:

   ```
   root@vmsrv01# umount /backup
   ```

   Now, confirm whether the volume is not found under the `df -h` command.

3. Next, we have to reduce the size of the filesystem:

   ```
   root@vmsrv01# lvreduce --resizefs --size 10G /dev/mygroup/backup
   ```

   ```
   fsck from util-linux 2.19.1
   /dev/mygroup/backup: clean,35/1310720 files, 60554/5242880 blocks
   resize2fs 1.40-WIP (14-Nov-2006)
   Resizing the filesystem on /dev/mygroup/
   backup to 2621440 (4k) blocks.
   The filesystem on /dev/mygroup/backup is now 2621440 blocks long.
   Reducing logical volume media to 10.00 GB
     Logical volume media successfully resized
   ```

    Make sure that your LV is formatted with a filesystem, for example, `ext4`, before using the `--resizefs` option. If not, it will fail and display the message `Bad magic number in super-block`.

4. The volume is reduced in size now, and we can mount it back to the system using the following command:

   ```
   root@vmsrv01# mount /dev/mygroup/backup /backup
   ```

5. To confirm that the volume is resized, we can use the `df -h` command:

   ```
   root@vmsrv01# df -h
   ```

   ```
   Filesystem               Size  Used Avail Use% Mounted on
   /dev/mygroup/backup      10G   236M  9.7G   2% /backup
   ```

6. Then, we can check the status of the LVM volume by issuing the following command:

```
root@vmsrv01# lvdisplay

LV Path                 /dev/mygroup/backup
LV Name                 backup
VG Name                 mygroup
LV Size                 10.0 GiB
```

Now, we should have some free extents in the volume group and be able to perform the snapshot. Another possible solution is to add an extra physical device to the volume group.

Adding/replacing physical storage for the existing LVM volume

Assume that we still have the preceding configuration and an additional physical device available at /dev/sdd1 with 10 GB of free space. Then, we can add this device to the volume group using the following steps:

1. At this moment, we can check the new status of the volume group using the following command:

```
root@vmsrv01# vgdisplay

VG Name                 mygroup
VG Size                 19.99 GiB
Total PE                5117
Alloc PE / Size         4096 / 16.00 GiB
Free  PE / Size         1021 / 3.99 GiB
```

2. Prepare the physical device to be converted to a physical volume in the LVM:

```
root@vmsrv01# pvcreate /dev/sdd1
```

3. Next, we can simply add this volume to our volume group (mygroup):

```
root@vmsrv01# vgextend mygroup /dev/sdd1
```

4. If you want to replace a physical volume (for example, /dev/sdc1) from the volume group, use the following command (this step is optional):

```
root@vmsrv01# pvmove /dev/sdc1 /dev/sdd1

/dev/sdc1: Moved: 1.9%
/dev/sdc1: Moved: 3.8%
...
/dev/sdc1: Moved: 100.0%
```

5. Then, remove the physical volume from the volume group with the following command:

```
root@vmsrv01# vgreduce mygroup /dev/sdc1
```

6. At this moment, we can check the new status of the volume group:

```
root@vmsrv01# vgdisplay

VG Name                mygroup
VG Size                29.99 GiB
Total PE               7676
Alloc PE / Size        4096 / 16.00 GiB
Free  PE / Size        3580 / 13.99 GiB
```

7. We have now allocated some free extents in our existing volume group (mygroup). Thus, we are able to create an LVM snapshot.

Backing up with vzdump and an LVM snapshot

Now, we are ready to perform a backup on a VM with zero downtime. Simply follow the ensuing steps to achieve it:

1. Log in to the target Proxmox server.

2. Issue the following command:

```
root@vmsrv01# vzdump -mode snapshot -dumpdir /backup \
-compress gzip 100

...
INFO: status = running
INFO: backup mode: snapshot
INFO: creating lvm snapshot of /dev/mapper/pve-data ('/dev/pve/
vzsnap-vmsrv01-0')
INFO: Logical volume "vzsnap-vmsrv01-0" created
INFO: creating archive '/backup/vzdump-
openvz-100-2014_07_05-16_30_56.tar.gz'
INFO: Total bytes written: 702310400 (670MiB, 6.4MiB/s)
INFO: archive file size: 247MB
INFO: Finished Backup of VM 100 (00:02:00)
INFO: Backup job finished successfully
```

We found that during the operation, an LVM snapshot, vzsnap-vmsrv01-0, is created at /dev/mapper/pve-data, as the data for the VM is stored under this directory. Besides, I have modified the command-line option to use -dumpdir instead of -storage; with this option, you can *specify the target directory directly* without the need to create a backup location under the web management console. Notice that the operation time is similar to the time we needed under the suspend mode. Therefore, it is the recommended method to back up an OpenVZ container.

3. By default, if the VM is in the *stop state*, vzdump will be operated in the *stop mode*, while it will be operated in the *snapshot mode* if the VM is running. So, you can remove the -mode snapshot option if your VM is running.

4. Don't forget to back up your configuration file using the following command:

```
root@vmsrv01# cp /etc/pve/nodes/vmsrv01/openvz/100.conf \ /backup/
dump/100.conf
```

If you think that it is difficult to remember all the parameters needed for a backup operation, you can simply define the default settings for vzdump in /etc/vzdump.conf.

We have gone through the backup procedures on both the OpenVZ containers and KVM machines under the command-line interface with the vzdump command. Shouldn't it be easier to make use of our web interface to perform a backup? Let's check this in the next section.

Backing up with the web management console

Apart from manually backing up the container using the command-line interface, we can also back it up using the web management interface. Here are the steps to back up the container with the help of the web management GUI:

1. Log in to the web management console using the root account information.

2. Browse to the left-hand side panel to locate the VM that needs to be backed up.

3. Choose the **Backup** tab from the right-hand side panel, and you will only see the latest backup files you created in the previous steps.

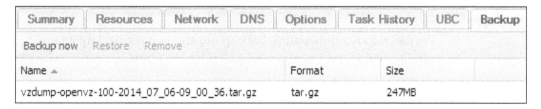

4. Then, we can simply click on the **Backup** button to start the backup dialog box, as shown in the following screenshot:

Notice that Proxmox uses the TAR package as the compression method and makes use of the **Snapshot** mode by default. Therefore, make sure you have enough free space in your VG that *stores the data of the VMs* before using the default values. By default, the volume group used is `pve`, which is mounted at `/var/lib/vz`, and you cannot place your dump file in the same VG.

5. From the dialog box, we can choose whether the backup output file should be compressed or not. To conserve disk space, we choose **GZIP** as the **Compression** method and choose a snapshot to enjoy a zero downtime backup process, as shown in the following screenshot:

6. If you follow my steps, the backup should be stopped with the following error, because we have defined that there should be only one backup per VM to be stored in our backup storage:

    ```
    ERROR: Backup of VM 100 failed - only 1 backup(s) allowed - please
    consider to remove old backup files.
    ```

    In this scenario, we have two options:

    ○   We can remove the existing backup file and run the backup again
    ○   We can redefine the backup storage to *allow more than one backup file*

    I will go for the second option for your reference.

7. Click on **Datacenter** in the left-hand side panel and choose the **Storage** tab from the right-hand side panel.

8. Find our backup storage, that is, **Backup**, and double-click on it. An **Edit: Directory** window appears, as shown in the following screenshot:

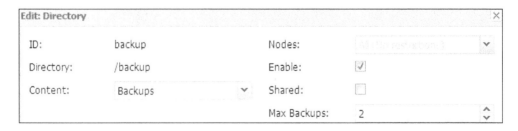

9. As you can see, the **Max Backups** value is set to 1. Now, we can change it to 2 and click on **OK**.

10. Get back to the backup page of VM 100 and click on the **Backup** button again. This time, we should be able to run the backup without any error.

11. A new backup file should be listed as follows:

Name ▲	Format	Size
vzdump-openvz-100-2014_07_05-16_44_41.tar.gz	tar.gz	247MB
vzdump-openvz-100-2014_07_05-22_56_19.tar.gz	tar.gz	247MB

This is the backup process for both OpenVZ containers and KVM machines. In the next section, we will go through the restore procedures of VMs.

The restore process of VMs in Proxmox

We have gone through different types of backup modes provided by the vzdump command and created different backup files for our VMs. However, we won't stop here because our target is to restore the VMs when there is a problem. This is the main reason we would like to perform a backup. Let's learn about it step by step.

Restoring a VM with vzrestore

In the previous section, we created our own backup files for VM 100 and VM 101 under /backup/dump. Now, it's time for us to practice restoring a VM from those backup files. We can restore the container with the vzrestore command or via the web management console. The following section shows the restore procedures when you choose to restore a VM using the command line with the vzrestore command.

Restoring an OpenVZ container with vzrestore

To avoid overwriting the existing VM data, we will restore it to VMID401. The steps for this are as follows:

1. Make sure that we have the backup file at /backup/dump. The filename might be different but should match the pattern mentioned earlier:

   ```
   vzdump-openvz-100-2014_07_06-09_05_14.tar.gz
   ```

2. Issue the `vzrestore` command with the following parameters:

```
root@vmsrv01# vzrestore \
/backup/dump/vzdump-openvz-100-2014_07_06-09_05_14.tar.gz 401

...
extracting archive '/backup/dump/vzdump-
openvz-100-2014_07_06-09_00_36.tar.gz'
Total bytes read: 703651840 (672MiB, 13MiB/s)
restore configuration to '/etc/pve/nodes/vmsrv01/openvz/401.conf'
```

As you can see, we don't need to copy the files manually because the `vzrestore` command does it for us. It will also create a configuration file in the right place (for example, at `/etc/pve/nodes/vmsrv01/openvz`) with the new VMID we have specified.

> If you want to overwrite an existing VM during the restore operation, issue the `vzrestore` command with the `-force` option:
>
> ```
> root@vmsrv01# vzrestore \
> /backup/dump/vzdump-openvz-100-2014_07_06-09_05_14.
> tar.gz 401 -force
> ```

3. We have to check whether the data is properly restored using the following command:

```
root@vmsrv01# ls /var/lib/vz/private/401

bin    dev  home  lib64       media  opt   root  selinux  sys  usr
boot   etc  lib   lost+found  mnt    proc  sbin  srv      tmp  var
```

4. Also, we would like to check whether the configuration is the same as VM 100:

```
root@vmsrv01# diff /etc/vz/conf/100.conf /etc/vz/conf/400.conf

38,39c38,39
< VE_ROOT="/var/lib/vz/root/$VEID"
< VE_PRIVATE="/var/lib/vz/private/100"
---
> VE_ROOT="/var/lib/vz/root/401"
> VE_PRIVATE="/var/lib/vz/private/401"
```

5. The new configuration of VM 401 is the same as that of VM 100, except for the values of the root and work directories of the VM.

6. It you run the new VM with the following command, you will receive an error that shows that the *IP address is already used*, as shown in the following command and its output:

```
root@vmsrv01# vzctl start 401
```

```
Starting container ...
Container is mounted
Adding IP address(es): 192.168.1.10
Unable to add IP 192.168.1.10: Address already in use
Container start failed (try to check kernel messages, e.g. "dmesg
| tail")
Killing container ...
Container was stopped
Container is unmounted
```

 By default, the `vzctl start` command doesn't check whether the IP address of the new container exists in the network. We can prevent this problem by editing the `/etc/vz/vz.conf` file with `ERROR_ON_ARPFAIL="yes"`.

7. Now, we need to modify the configuration file at `/etc/pve/nodes/vmsrv01/401.conf` using the following command:

   root@vmsrv01# nano /etc/pve/nodes/vmrv01/401.conf

8. Change the value of `IP_ADDRESS` using the following command:

   ```
   from: IP_ADDRESS="192.168.1.10"
   to:   IP_ADDRESS="192.168.1.41"
   ```

   You might also need to change the value of the `HOSTNAME` field:

   ```
   from: HOSTNAME="myvm1.localdomain"
   to:   HOSTNAME="myvm1-1.localdomain"
   ```

9. Then, we should be able to start the container without any problem, as shown in the following command and its output:

   root@vmsrv01# vzctl start 401

   ```
   Starting container ...
   Initializing quota ...
   Container is mounted
   Adding IP address(es): 192.168.1.41
   Setting CPU units: 1000
   Setting CPUs: 1
   Container start in progress...
   ```

   We can check whether it is running using the `vzlist` command:

   root@vmsrv01# vzlist

   ```
   CTID  NPROC STATUS     IP_ADDR         HOSTNAME
    401   17   running    192.168.1.41    myvm1-1.localdomain
   ```

We can also use the `ping` command:

```
root@vmsrv01# ping 192.168.1.41
```

We can also access the VM with the `vzctl` command:

```
root@vmsrv01# vzctl enter 401
```

10. Inside the backup page of the web management console, the source backup files are now being treated as the backup files for the new VM, as shown in the following screenshot:

	Name ▲	Format	Size
100 (myvm1.localdomain)			
102 (test.localdomain)	vzdump-openvz-100-2014_07_06-09_00_36.tar.gz	tar.gz	247MB
202 (gtest01.localdomain)	vzdump-openvz-100-2014_07_06-09_05_14.tar.gz	tar.gz	247MB
401 (myvm1.localdomain)			

We have finished restoring the OpenVZ container. Next, we will check the procedures on how to restore a KVM machine with the `vzdump` backup files.

Restoring a KVM machine with vzrestore

To avoid overwriting the existing virtual machine data, we will now restore it to VMID402. The steps to do this are as follows:

1. Make sure we have the backup file at /backup/dump:

   ```
   vzdump-qemu-101-2014_07_05-23_36_29.vma
   ```

2. Issue the `vzrestore` command to restore from the backup file:

   ```
   root@vmsrv01# vzrestore \
   /backup/dump/vzdump-qemu-101-2014_07_06-09_40_32.vma.gz  402

   ...
   extracting archive '/backup/dump/vzdump-
   qemu-101-2014_07_06-09_40_32.vma.gz'
   tar: This does not look like a tar archive
   tar: Skipping to next header
   Total bytes read: 10240 (10KiB, 18MiB/s)
   tar: Exiting with failure status due to previous errors
   command 'tar xpf /backup/dump/vzdump-qemu-101-2014_07_06-09_40_32.
   vma.gz --totals --sparse -C /var/lib/vz/private/402' failed: exit
   code 2
   ```

3. From the output result, we know that the `vzrestore` command requires a `tar` package instead of a VMA file. To restore a KVM machine, we need to use the `qmrestore` command instead:

   ```
   root@vmsrv01# qmrestore \
   ```

```
/backup/dump/vzdump-qemu-101-2014_07_06-09_40_32.vma.gz   402
...
restore vma archive: zcat /backup/dump/vzdump-
qemu-101-2014_07_06-09_40_32.vma.gz|vma extract -v -r /var/tmp/
vzdumptmp667708.fifo - /var/tmp/vzdumptmp667708
CFG: size: 236 name: qemu-server.conf
DEV: dev_id=1 size: 8589934592 devname: drive-ide0
CTIME: Sun Jul  6 09:40:33 2014
Formatting '/var/lib/vz/images/402/vm-402-disk-1.qcow2', fmt=qcow2
size=8589934592 encryption=off cluster_size=65536
reallocation='metadata' lazy_refcounts=off
new volume ID is 'local:402/vm-402-disk-1.qcow2'
map 'drive-ide0' to '/var/lib/vz/images/402/vm-402-disk-1.qcow2'
(write zeros = 0)
progress 1% (read 85917696 bytes, duration 0 sec)
...
progress 100% (read 8589934592 bytes, duration 32 sec)
```

If you want to overwrite the existing VM during a restore operation, issue the qmrestore command with the -force option:

**root@vmsrv01# qmrestore **

/backup/dump/vzdump-

qemu-101-2014_07_06-09_40_32.vma.gz 402 -force

4. During the operation, the following two files are created:

    ° The configuration file at /etc/pve/qemu-server/402.conf

    ° The disk image at /var/lib/vz/images/402/vm-402-disk-1.qcow2

5. We can further check whether the configuration file is the same as the original one using the following command:

    root@vmsrv01# diff /etc/pve/qemu-server/402.conf /etc/pve/qemu-server/101.conf

    ```
    ...
    3c3
    < ide0: local:402/vm-402-disk-1.qcow2,size=8G
    ---
    > ide0: local:101/vm-101-disk-1.qcow2,format=qcow2,size=8G
    ```

    The only difference is the stored directory and the file name of the disk image.

6. Before turning on the new VM, make sure that you change the network settings by editing the configuration file or with the web management GUI to avoid service interruption.

7. Then, we can start the VM to see whether it works:

```
root@vmsrv01# qm start 402
```

8. You can check the current status of VM 402 with the `qm` command:

```
root@vmsrv01# qm list
VMID NAME      STATUS      MEM(MB)    BOOTDISK(GB) PID
402 testvm     running     512               8.00 673765
```

9. Inside the **Backup** page of the web management console, the source backup files are now being treated as the backup files for the new VM, as listed in the following screenshot, just like what we found in the OpenVZ container restoration:

402 (testvm)	Name ▲	Format	Size
	vzdump-qemu-101-2014_07_06-09_40_32.vma.gz	vma.gz	444MB

Now, we have gone over the steps to restore a VM for an OpenVZ container and a KVM machine under the **Command Line Interface** (**CLI**). If you are not comfortable with the CLI, we can do the same thing via the web management console.

Restoring a VM with the web management console

Besides restoring from a command-line interface, Proxmox provides a graphical interface for the user to finish a regular task easily. This method is suitable for both an OpenVZ container and KVM machine. The following steps demonstrate how we can perform such a task:

1. Log in to the web management console with the root account. Find your target virtual machine, for example, VM **100**, from the left-hand side menu and choose **Backup** from the right-hand side panel. You should be able to view the backup files that currently exist, as shown in the following screenshot:

You can even browse the content of the backup storage by choosing **vmsrv01**, selecting **Backup** from the left-hand side panel, and then selecting **Content** from the right-hand side panel. You can also list out all the backup files inside the storage, as shown in the following screenshot:

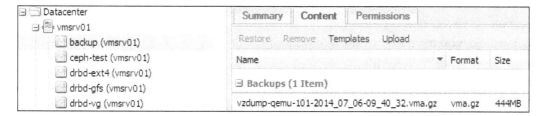

2. Click on the most recent backup and then choose **Restore** from the menu above it. A window named **Restore CT** is shown. You can change the **VM ID** if you don't want to use the default one.

3. A warning message stating that the existing VM data will be overwritten is shown:

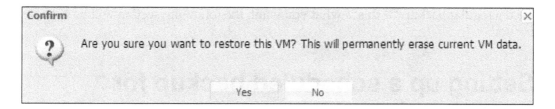

4. If your VM is running, you will get following dialog box for an OpenVZ container:

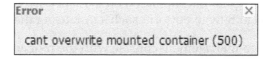

5. For a KVM machine, you will get the following dialog box:

6. So, you have to turn the VM off and restore it again. For OpenVZ, you have
    the following progress log:

```
you choose to force overwriting VPS config file, private and root
directories.
extracting archive '/backup/dump/vzdump-
openvz-100-2014_07_06-09_05_14.tar.gz'
restore configuration to '/etc/pve/nodes/vmsrv01/openvz/100.conf'
```

For the KVM, you have the following progress log:

```
restore vma archive: zcat /backup/dump/vzdump-
qemu-101-2014_07_06-09_40_32.vma.gz|vma extract -v -r /var/tmp/
vzdumptmp846694.fifo - /var/tmp/vzdumptmp846694
...
map 'drive-ide0' to '/var/lib/vz/images/101/vm-101-disk-1.qcow2'
(write zeros = 0)
progress 1% (read 85917696 bytes, duration 0 sec)
progress 100% (read 8589934592 bytes, duration 31 sec)
```

As you can see, the restoration also overwrites the VM configuration file. So, if you
have done some modifications on the configuration file after your backup operation,
you should properly *make a copy of your updated configuration file before running the
restoration process.*

Now, you have successfully backed up and restored your VM manually. What if you
need a regular backup? If this is what you want, the following section will be suitable
for you.

Setting up a scheduled backup for the VMs

In the previous section, we learned the procedures to restore a VM with backup files
under both the command-line and the graphic interfaces. Proxmox provides you with
the ability to perform a regular backup based on the schedule you have configured.
Let's take a further look at how to perform such a task using the following steps:

1. Log in to the web management console with the root account details.

2. Click on **Datacenter** and then choose **Backup** from the right-hand side panel, as shown in the following screenshot:

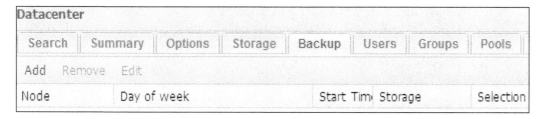

3. Click on the **Add** button; a window named **Create: Backup Job** is displayed, as shown in the following screenshot:

4. As an example, we will back up all the VMs that run under Proxmox, and it's better to compress the output file every **Sunday** morning at **01:00**. The backup configuration will be as shown in the following screenshot:

Note that you can even specify an e-mail address for notifications on the backup status.

5. If we have an important VM (for example, VM 100) that needs to be backed up every day, we can create a separate backup task to include multiple days to perform the backup operation, as shown in the following screenshot (this step is optional):

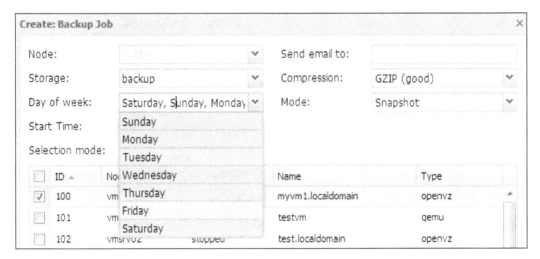

6. Click on **Create** to make a new backup schedule, and you should have the newly created backup task in your list, as shown in the following screenshot:

Node	Day of week	Start Time	Storage	Selection
vmsrv01	sun	01:00	backup	-- All --

Note that the backup files created by Proxmox are *full backups*; therefore, *you need to consider whether there is enough space to save your backup files*. If you are interested in making differential and incremental backups, check out these links:

- *KVM incremental backup* at `http://wiki.qemu.org/Features/Livebackup`
- *Proxmox differential backup* at `http://ayufan.eu/projects/proxmox-ve-differential-backups/`

As we can fit the system into a single package, would you be interested to see whether we can create a system template and deploy it afterwards? If yes, the next section is made for you.

Building up our own OS template

We introduced the concept of an OS template in *Chapter 1, Basic Concepts of a Proxmox Virtual Environment,* and uploaded a predefined template downloaded from the Internet. There are two types of templates; one is the OpenVZ template and the other one is the VM template:

- **OpenVZ template**: This is only used to build OpenVZ containers but not for a KVM machine. This limits the choice of operating system to a Linux platform.

- **VM template**: This was introduced with the Proxmox 3.x series, and is used to deploy a KVM's VM. This, therefore, escapes from the limitation of an operating system.

To begin with, we can make a move to check out how to build an OpenVZ template first.

Building our own OpenVZ template from an existing container

First, we need to have a running container, and I would like to pick VM 100 as our example. Then, follow the ensuing steps:

1. Enter the container to install any software you need using the following command:

   ```
   root@vmsrv01# vzctl enter 100
   ```

2. After you have finished installing the software, remember to clear the system caches. For example, if you are using yum to install software, then use the following command:

   ```
   root@myvm1# yum clean all
   ```

3. Also, we need to remove the network-related settings using the following command:

   ```
   root@myvm1# echo "" > /etc/resolv.conf
   ```

4. Remove the hostname settings for the VM:

   For CentOS, remove the `hostname` value at `/etc/sysconfig/network`

   For Debian, remove the hostname value at `rm -f /etc/hostname`

5. Stop the VM before we can make a template file using the following command:

   ```
   root@vmsrv01# vzctl stop 100
   ```

6. Then, remove the network configuration of the OpenVZ container using the following command:

    ```
    root@vmsrv01# vzctl set 100 --ipdel all --save
    ```

7. Change the directory to `/var/lib/vz/private/<VMID>`:

    ```
    root@vmsrv01# cd /var/lib/vz/private/100
    ```

8. Then, we have to decide the name of the template file. We must follow the naming pattern that is shown here:

    ```
    <OS>-<OSVERSION>-<NAME>_<VERSION>_<ARCH>.tar.gz
    ```

    For the `ARCH` value, use `i386` for a 32-bit platform and `amd64` for a 64-bit platform.

9. For example, if I am running on a CentOS 6.4 64-bit platform and installed a web server, I will have the following name:

    ```
    centos-6.4-web_6.4_amd64.tar.gz
    ```

10. When we are ready, pack the folder while excluding any temporary folders and custom mount points, and save it to the template directory:

    ```
    root@vmsrv01:/var/lib/vz/private/100# tar --numeric-owner -czf
    /var/lib/vz/template/cache/centos-6.4-web_6.4_amd64.tar.gz
    --exclude=tmp/* --exclude=lost+found/ .
    ```

11. When the operation is finished, we can log in to the web management console, choose **vmsrv01**, and find the **Local** storage. Then, choose **Content** from the right-hand side panel. Under the **Templates** section, you will be able to see your newly created template available for use, as shown in the following screenshot:

Summary	Content	Permissions	
Restore Remove Templates Upload			
Name		Format	Size
⊞ Images (1 Item)			
⊞ ISO (3 Items)			
⊟ Templates (2 Items)			
centos-6-x86_64-devel.tar.gz		tgz	249MB
centos-6-x86_64-web.tar.gz		tgz	249MB

12. Now, we can try to build a new VM with our own template. Make sure you have chosen the right Proxmox server that contains your custom template file, because the custom template file is not published throughout the cluster. When you choose **Template** from the container-creation window, you can choose your own template, as shown in the following screenshot:

You might be wondering how the operation can be completed even if we haven't created a configuration file for our new VM. This is because there are default configuration files under `/etc/vz/dists` that include well-known Linux distributions. Therefore, we must follow the naming criteria when we create our own template. This template-creation process is based on CentOS. If you are creating templates for other operating systems, check out the following links:

- **Debian**: `https://openvz.org/Debian_template_creation`
- **Ubuntu**: `https://openvz.org/Ubuntu_Gutsy_template_creation`

Building our own VM template from an existing KVM machine

Like the OS template concept in an OpenVZ container, KVM also provides a template function named the VM template. To build with this template, we need to have a running KVM. We can make use of VM 101 for testing.

 Note that when you convert a KVM into a template, you won't be able to start it again without building a new VM based on it.

The following steps will help you while building your own VM template from an existing KVM:

1. As usual, install the required software on the template operating system.

2. When finished, remove all the user data, passwords, and keys (for example, SSH keys) from the operating system. This part will not be explained in more detail. To learn how to do this for a Windows platform, you can check out `http://technet.microsoft.com/en-us/library/ee523217%28v=ws.10%29.aspx`.

3. Then, right-click on the VM and choose **Convert to template**, as shown in the following screenshot:

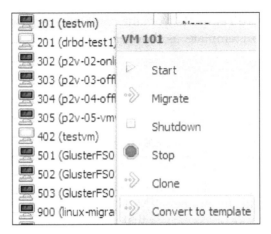

4. Click on **Yes** when a confirmation prompt is shown.

5. When the operation is finished, the icon of VM 101 changes, indicating that it is a template rather than a standard VM and you won't be able to turn it on.

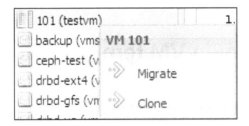

At this time, we can perform the following types of operations on the VM template:

*   **Migrate**: This simply moves the selected template file from one Proxmox server to another

*   **Clone**: In the clone mode, there are two different options:

    *   **Full clone**: This is used to create a complete separate copy of the original template file, and it requires the same disk space as the original.

    *   **Linked clone**: This uses up less space but cannot run without the original VM template file. Besides, it doesn't work with the LVM and iSCSI storages.

Therefore, if you are using the *Linked clone* option to conserve disk space, you have to remember *not* to move/migrate the original VM template file, as the linked clone image will record all the changes made after the base image has been created. For more information on full clone versus linked clone, check out the following link:

```
https://www.vmware.com/support/ws5/doc/ws_clone_overview.html
```

If we choose to use the linked clone mode, the configuration file for the hard disk will be different, as shown in the following screenshot:

Hard Disk (ide0)	local: 101/base-101-disk-1.qcow2/103/vm-103-disk-1.qcow2,format=qcow2,size=8G

The disk image size is slightly smaller than the original one. The size can be checked with the following command:

```
root@vmsrv01# ls -lah /var/lib/vz/images/103
-rw-r--r--  1 root root 193K Jul  7 00:38 vm-103-disk-1.qcow2
```

On the other hand, in the full clone mode, the size will be the same as the normal one:

Hard Disk (ide0)	local: 104/vm-104-disk-1.qcow2,format=qcow2,size=8G

The new disk image size is the same as the original one:

```
root@vmsrv01# ls -lah /var/lib/vz/images/104
-rw-r--r--  1 root root 8.1G Jul  7 00:38 vm-104-disk-1.qcow2
```

Therefore, we have gone through the process of creating system templates on both the OpenVZ containers and KVMs. It will now be much easier if we need to build similar VMs with the same operating system.

Up to this stage, we have learned how to set up our own backup schedule to protect our VMs. We also know the procedures of VM restoration. What if a cluster member, (a Proxmox server in our case) fails? Is there any way to replace the existing server with another one? I am going to show you how to solve the problem of a single cluster node failure and rebuild a failed cluster.

System recovery of a Proxmox cluster failure

Normally, the cluster can be automatically recovered from a cluster node after a network or system failure. However, when you need to upgrade or replace the existing cluster node, we have to follow the procedures listed in the following sections to make it work.

Replacing a failed cluster node

In this case, you probably have one broken machine inside your cluster. When you log in to the web management console, you might see that the status of the broken cluster node *turns red* and shows that the node is *not online*; this can be seen on the **Summary** page under **Datacenter**. Assume that the broken machine is **vmsrv02**, as shown in the following screenshot:

When you check the status of the cluster with the `clustat` command, you will get the following result:

```
root@vmsrv01# clustat

Member Name             ID    Status
------ ----            ----  ------
 vmsrv01                1     Online, Local, rgmanager
 vmsrv02                2     Offline
 /dev/block/8:16        0     Online, Quorum Disk
```

Another problem is that all your non-HA enabled VMs under **vmsrv02** are unable to start. According to the backup files you have, the repair steps are different. Let's check out how to perform the repair process in the following steps. For more information on the installation steps of different components, refer to *Chapter 4, Configuring a Proxmox VE Cluster*:

1. Turn off your failed machine. Fortunately, our cluster is able to bear one cluster node failure. So, we can simply remove the failure node from the cluster with the `pvecm` command, as shown in the following command:

   ```
   root@vmsrv01# pvecm delnode vmsrv02
   ```

2. After that, you can perform a brand new installation on your new Proxmox server. Make sure that you have installed the DRBD and GlusterFS packages. Copy all files at `/etc/drbd.d` for the DRBD configurations of `vmsrv01` to `vmsrv02`. Configure all the storage devices, for example, the *DRBD* storage and *GlusterFS* storages, in `vmsrv02`.

3. If you have used *CEPH* as the storage for a VM, you can copy the configuration files from `vmsrv01` to `/etc/pve/ceph.conf`.

4. The mount points associated with them should be properly defined in Proxmox, because you have to restore the `storage.cfg` file to `vmsrv02`.

   If you don't have `storage.cfg` on your backup media, you can simply copy the file from `/etc/pve/storage.cfg` in `vmsrv01` to `vmsrv02`.

5. If you have done everything well, you should see all the storages as shown in the following screenshot:

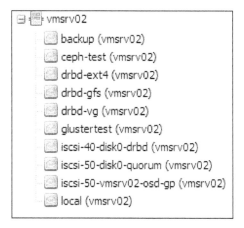

6. Make sure that you can properly view the status of your storages. For example, the DRBD storage should look as shown in the following screenshot:

7. After your storage configurations are restored, we can restore the VMs to resume normal operation. If you have backed up the content with the following folders, you can simply restore the VM by copying the following files to vmsrv02:

   ○ /etc/pve/nodes/vmsrv02/openvz/

   ○ /etc/pve/nodes/vmsrv02/qemu-server/

   ○ /var/lib/vz/private/

   ○ /var/lib/vz/images/

   If you have only the following VM backup files, then you need to restore your VMs one by one with the web management console. Refer to the *Restoring a virtual machine with the web management console* section for more information:

   ○ vzdump-openvz-100-2014_07_04-16_12_05.tar.gz

   ○ vzdump-qemu-101-2014_07_05-23_36_29.vma.gz

8. Try to start your VMs one by one after the VMs have recovered, to check whether there is any problem.

9. If there is no problem when running the VMs, check whether the *quorum disk* is available to vmsrv02 (no need to rebuild it) before you add it back to the cluster, as shown in the following screenshot:

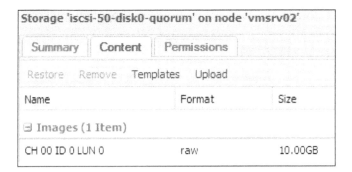

10. Issue the pvecm command on vmsrv02 to join the server back to the cluster:

    root@vmsrv02# pvecm add vmsrv01

11. Now, you should be able to see `vmsrv02` on the web management page, as shown in the following screenshot:

Here, we learned how to recover a failed node from the backup files. What if we want to build an identical cluster system for service redundancy? There are many preparations that need to be performed, and detailed steps have been provided for your reference in the following section.

Building a redundant cluster from the backup files

First of all, we need to back up all the VMs and cluster-related configuration files. Then, use the following files as your source files for the new cluster:

1. The first thing we need to back up is the following cluster configuration file:
   - `/etc/pve/cluster.conf`

2. If you want to have an identical system, then you need to copy the following authorization key, which is used by the Proxmox server to perform configuration synchronization (this step is optional):
   - `/etc/pve/authkey.key`

3. Back up the following configuration file, which keeps all the storage information listed in the cluster source page:
   - `/etc/pve/storage.cfg`

4. As we need to have the iSCSI storage to be our quorum disk, back up the iSCSI configuration file too:
   - `/etc/iscsi/iscsid.conf`

5. If you also need to back up the settings for the iSCSI server, then you can refer to `http://goo.gl/iFGphj`.

6. If you have enabled the CEPH service, you also need to copy the following files:

    ° `/etc/pve/priv/ceph.conf`

    ° `/etc/pve/priv/ceph.client.admin.keyring`

    ° `/etc/pve/priv/ceph.mon.keyring`

7. Moreover, back up the following DRBD configuration files:

    ° `/etc/drbd.d/*`

    ° `/etc/drbd.conf`

8. If you have defined your default settings for the `vzdump` command, then you need to back up the following file:

    ° `/etc/vzdump.conf`

9. If you have created a scheduled backup, then you need to copy the following file to every cluster node for which you have scheduled backup tasks:

    ° `/etc/pve/vzdump.cron`

10. You might also need to copy your custom OS and OpenVZ templates that are at the following location:

    ° `/var/lib/vz/template/cache/*`

11. You might also need to copy the ISO files that you needed for the operating system installation with the KVM machine:

    ° `/var/lib/vz/template/iso/*`

12. Furthermore, back up the configuration file to define a system mount point at startup:

    ° `/etc/fstab`

13. You might have custom cron jobs to clear log files; in which case, you also need to back them up:

    ° `/etc/crontab`

14. If you are using an LVM storage, you need to back it up too:

    ° `/etc/lvm/lvm.conf`

    Remember to back up the settings for the LVM devices with the `vgcfgbackup` command. You can refer to *Chapter 6, System Migration of an Existing System to a Proxmox VE Cluster.*

15. Of course, you need to back up all the VMs; for this, refer to the previous section, *Back up process for VMs in Proxmox*.

16. Don't forget to copy your network configuration file from every cluster node at the `vmsrv01.interfaces` path; you can identify the files with names such as:

    ○ `/etc/network/interfaces`

    ○ `/etc/hosts`

    ○ `/etc/hostname`

17. For the network part, we need to back up the switch configuration too. Since I am using a Cisco product, refer to the following link for more information about it:

    `http://www.cisco.com/c/en/us/support/docs/ios-nx-os-software/`
    `ios-software-releases-122-mainline/46741-backup-config.html`

    If you are not using a Cisco product, search for the backup method available for your product.

18. If you have created a Gluster filesystem on separate machines, you need to back up the directory that you have exported for Proxmox to use. In my case, it would be `/glusterfs-data/*`.

19. Save the firewall rules used by `iptables` separately using the following commands:

    ```
    root@glusterFS1# iptables-save > glusterFS1.iptables
    root@glusterFS2# iptables-save > glusterFS2.iptables
    root@glusterFS3# iptables-save > glusterFS3.iptables
    ```

    You can restore the configurations afterwards with the following commands:

    ```
    root@glusterFS1# iptables-restore < glusterFS1.iptables
    root@glusterFS2# iptables-restore < glusterFS2.iptables
    root@glusterFS3# iptables-restore < glusterFS3.iptables
    ```

With all the configurations in hand, you can follow the instructions to install all the software packages by referring to *Chapter 4, Configuring a Proxmox VE Cluster,* and restore the configurations to your new machines to form an identical cluster as a redundancy system to be used in case of an emergency.

We have gone through the topics on how to rebuild/recover our cluster system. If we want to remove Proxmox from a cluster node to free up a server for some other use, what will be the right procedure that will not affect the cluster? This is covered in the following section.

Removing a cluster member node

For this kind of operation, I would suggest that you create backup files on all the VMs that run under the affected server. If you are running a two-node cluster, it is recommended that you add another Proxmox server (for example, vmsrv03) to the cluster to avoid a single point of failure.

Next, make sure that you have moved all the VMs that run under the affected server to prevent any system service downtime with the following steps:

1. Log in to the web management console of the cluster's main server, for example, vmsrv01.

2. Browse to the affected server (for example, vmsrv02), right-click on the VMs, and choose **Migrate**.

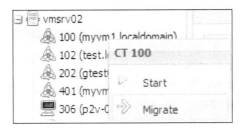

3. Migrate to a cluster node other than vmsrv02 (for example, vmsrv01) and click on **Migrate**.

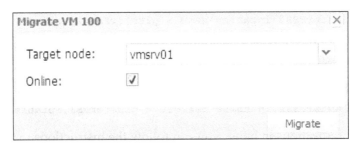

4. Perform the preceding steps on all the VMs that run under vmsrv02.

   When there is no VM that runs under the affected server, you are ready to remove the cluster information on your machine, for example, vmsrv02.

5. Now, you are free to remove the node from vmsrv01 using the following command:

   ```
   root@vmsrv01# pvecm delnode vmsrv02
   ```

6. When we check the cluster status using the following command, there is no vmsrv02 inside:

```
root@vmsrv01# clustat

Member Name                ID     Status
------- ----              ----   ------
 vmsrv01                   1      Online, Local, rgmanager
 /dev/block/8:16           0      Online, Quorum Disk
```

7. After that, we need to stop the Proxmox cluster filesystem (pmxcfs) service that contains the corosync service on vmsrv02. This will also unmount the Proxmox system mount point at /etc/pve:

```
root@vmsrv02# /etc/init.d/pve-cluster stop
```

8. Stop the cluster manager service using the following command:

```
root@vmsrv02# /etc/init.d/cman stop
```

9. To ensure that the service is properly turned off, issue the kill command:

```
root@vmsrv02# killall -9 corosync cman dlm_controld fenced
```

10. Remove the cluster configuration files using the following command:

```
root@vmsrv02# rm /etc/cluster/cluster.conf
root@vmsrv02# rm -rf /var/lib/pve-cluster/*
root@vmsrv02# rm -rf /var/lib/cluster/*
```

Make sure you are *not* removing the cluster directory itself. If you remove the cluster directory, you will be unable to start the pve-cluster service, which means you cannot mount the main Proxmox configuration directory, /etc/pve.

11. Check whether pve-cluster can be started using the following command:

```
root@vmsrv02# /etc/init.d/pve-cluster start
```

12. Perform a system reboot after the removal.

13. When you log in to the web management console of vmsrv02 again, you should not see the other cluster node. Then, you can safely remove this machine from the cluster farm.

Summary

In this chapter, we learned how to perform a backup and restore of our VMs. As a good habit, I introduced how to create our own backup schedules for our system. If we encounter a system failure during daily operation, we now know the procedures to recover the failed node in our cluster. If the system is unrecoverable, we know how to remove it safely without affecting the production system. Finally, I introduced the configuration files needed if we want to build the cluster from the beginning.

In the next chapter, we will go through some problems I encountered during the system installation and how we can solve them. I hope it will be a good reference for you.

8
Troubleshooting on a Proxmox Cluster

Up to this point, we have acquired all the knowledge necessary to build our own Proxmox cluster. In case you encounter any problem during the operation, I have prepared this chapter to share the difficulties I faced during the creation of this book and the solutions to fix the problems. For your convenience, the problems are summarized into different categories listed as follows:

- System access problems
- System migration problems
- System storage problems
- Cluster system problems

First, let's start with the display problems that you might face when you use a Proxmox system.

Troubleshooting system access problems

Now, it should not be difficult for you to install a new Proxmox server from scratch. However, after I performed a few installations on different platforms, I noticed that there were a few scenarios that might cause you trouble. The problems I found are discussed in the following sections.

Undefined video mode number

Symptom: In some motherboards, you will receive the *Undefined video mode number* warning after you press *Enter* to begin the installation. It simply tells you that you cannot run the fancy installation wizard, as shown in the following screenshot:

```
Press Return to install Proxmox Virtual Environment.
Proxmox VE 3.2 (build 5a885216-5) - http://www.proxmox.com/

boot:
Undefined video mode number: 317
```

Root cause: The main problem is the display chipset. When your motherboard is using a display chipset that is not VESA 2.0-compatible, this error message appears. To learn more about VESA 2.0, visit the following links:

- *VESA BIOS Extensions* on Wikipedia: http://goo.gl/dODlKj
- A Proxmox forum thread that describes the installation problem: http://goo.gl/qnFgP3

Solution: You will be asked to press *Enter* or the Space bar, or wait for 30 seconds to continue. If you have pressed *Enter*, the possible video modes available on your system will be displayed, as shown in the following screenshot:

```
Press <ENTER> to see video modes available, <SPACE> to continue, or wait 30 sec
Mode: Resolution:    Type: Mode: Resolution:    Type: Mode: Resolution:    Type:
0 F00    80x25       UGA   1 F01    80x50       UGA   2 F02    80x43       UGA
3 F03    80x28       UGA   4 F05    80x30       UGA   5 F06    80x34       UGA
6 F07    80x60       UGA   7 300   640x400x8    VESA  8 301   640x480x8    VESA
9 303   800x600x8    VESA  a 30E   320x200x16   VESA  b 311   640x480x16   VESA
c 314   800x600x16   VESA  d 320   320x200x8    VESA  e 321   320x400x8    VESA
f 322   640x400x8    VESA  g 323   640x480x8    VESA  h 324   800x600x8    VESA
i 32E   320x200x16   VESA  j 32F   320x400x16   VESA  k 330   640x400x16   VESA
l 331   640x480x16   VESA  m 332   800x600x16   VESA  n 33C   320x200x32   VESA
o 33D   320x400x32   VESA  p 33E   640x400x32   VESA  q 33F   640x480x32   VESA
r 340   800x600x32   VESA  s 356   320x240x8    VESA  t 357   320x240x16   VESA
u 358   320x240x32   VESA  v 359   400x300x8    VESA  w 35A   400x300x16   VESA
x 35B   400x300x32   VESA  y 35C   512x384x8    VESA  z 35D   512x384x16   VESA
  35E   512x384x32   VESA    36E   720x480x8    VESA    36F   720x480x16   VESA
  370   720x480x32   VESA    371   720x576x8    VESA    372   720x576x16   VESA
  373   720x576x32   VESA    374   800x480x8    VESA    375   800x480x16   VESA
  376   800x480x32   VESA
Enter a video mode or "scan" to scan for additional modes:
```

You can pick up a display mode number based on the list shown in this screenshot. Normally, you can select the *display mode* 314 *that has* 800x600 *resolution and a 16-bit color depth*, or you can choose the *display mode* 311, *which provides you with a* 640x480 *resolution and a 16-bit color depth*. Now, you should be able to continue with the installation process.

Prevention: I found that this problem normally happened with Nvidia display cards. If possible, you can try to replace the Nvidia card with an Intel or an ATI display card for your installation.

Cannot open the console window in the web management GUI

Symptom: If we want to display the system console window for one VM under Proxmox, a Java-based applet program is executed as the viewer to interact with the getty service, which exports the system terminal (TTY1) to the user when there is a connection.

By default, the system terminal is not exported to the user. To do that, you have to follow the instructions provided in the *Accessing a new VM* section of *Chapter 1, Basic Concepts of a Proxmox Virtual Environment*. When you try to access the VM properly, you might receive the following message on the screen:

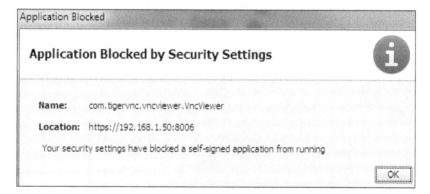

Root cause: This error simply indicates that your current security settings in the Java runtime environment are not allowing the Java applet to run, and you cannot allow it exclusively at this stage. You can visit the following link to learn more about the error:

How do I control when an untrusted applet or application runs in my web browser?: http://goo.gl/2P277z.

Solution: Therefore, to access our system console, we need to change the setting using these steps:

1. If, like me, you are running a Windows-based client, access your Java Control Panel, that is, Java (32-bit), through the **System Settings** option from **Control Panel**.

2. Inside the **Java Control Panel**, select **Security**. The default security level should be set to **High**, as shown in the following screenshot:

3. Next, you need to add the IP address for the Proxmox server as an exception site to allow Java applet execution. Choose **Edit Site List** from the window:

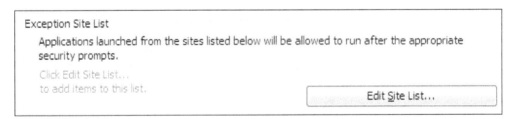

4. Click on **Add** and enter https://192.168.1.57:8006 in the list, as shown in the following screenshot:

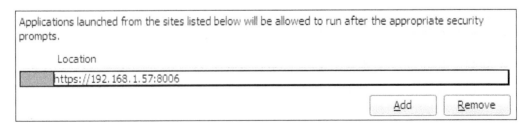

5. Click on **OK** and the website is added to the **Exception Site List**, as shown in the following screenshot:

Exception Site List

Applications launched from the sites listed below will be allowed to run after the appropriate security prompts.

https://192.168.1.57:8006

6. When you try to launch the console window of a VM, you will now be able to see the following option that allows execution of the Java applet:

Select the box below, then click Run to start the application

☑ I accept the risk and want to run this application.   [Run]   [Cancel]

Prevention: We cannot prevent this error as it is the default setting that Java uses to protect us from harmful applets. Just allowing our applet to run will solve the problem.

A KVM machine cannot be turned off using the Shutdown command

Symptom: This issue occurs if you want to turn off a Linux-based VM with the **Shutdown** command via a web management console, as shown in the following screenshot:

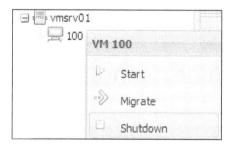

However, you find that the Shutdown command is executed with the following output:

```
TASK ERROR: VM quit/powerdown failed - got timeout
```

Root cause: The error appears because Proxmox uses an ACPI signal to turn off the VM, and the ACPI-related packages might not be installed in the Linux-based template. So, the VM cannot be normally shut down via the GUI console.

Solution: In this case, you need to perform the following operations inside the Linux-based VM:

1. Install the ACPI daemon service with the yum command:

   ```
   root@myvm1# yum -y install acpid
   ```

2. Start the ACPI daemon service:

   ```
   root@myvm1# service acpid start
   ```

3. Enable auto startup for the ACPI service during system startup:

   ```
   root@myvm1# chkconfig acpid on
   ```

Prevention: You can build a customized Linux template that includes the ACPI daemon to avoid this problem.

These are the main problems I have encountered during the setup process with the HA environment. In the next section, I will mention some of the problems that might occur during system migration.

Troubleshooting system migration problems

With reference to *Chapter 6, System Migration of an Existing System to a Proxmox VE Cluster*, we ran through all the steps to perform system migration. However, there are some minor configurations that will cause the migration process to fail.

The KVM machine cannot be migrated

Symptom: When you try to move your existing KVM machine from one server to another, you might encounter the following error:

```
ERROR: Failed to sync data - can't migrate local cdrom 'local:iso/CentOS-
6.5-x86_64-minimal.iso'
aborting phase 1 - cleanup resources
```

Root cause: This is a common mistake, especially if you want to move your KVM image after you have finished installing the operating system under your VM. The local mounted ISO image cannot be found in the target Proxmox server, and synchronizing this ISO image from the source to the target server also fails. Therefore, Proxmox stops this operation to avoid any data loss.

Solution: To solve this problem, we have two possible approaches: remove the mounted ISO file from the CD-ROM entry or move the ISO file manually from the source server to the target server. To remove the CD-ROM entry, you need to change the content of the VM configuration file manually in the path `/etc/pve/nodes/<proxmox_hostname>/<VMID>.conf`.

For example, we have the following entry:

`ide2: local:iso/CentOS-6.5-x86_64-minimal.iso,media=cdrom`

`Change the value to: ide2: none,media=cdrom`

Of course, you can make such a change in the web management console too, using the following steps:

1. Choose the VM from the left panel, then choose the **Hardware** tab from the right panel, and locate the **CD/DVD Drive** entry:

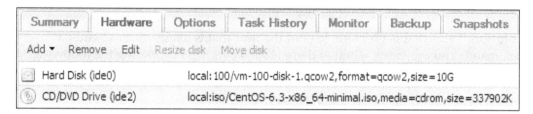

2. Double-click on the **CD/DVD Drive** entry or click on **Edit** from the top menu, and choose **Do not use any media** from the **Edit** window:

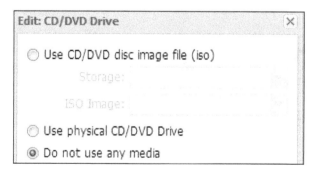

3. Rerun the migrate operation again, and you should now be free from the error.

Prevention: Make sure you remember to disable the localized settings (for example, CD/DVD drives, mounted ISO, and so on) before performing system migration.

An OpenVZ container cannot be migrated

Symptom: Similar to the migration problem with the KVM VM, we also have a chance of encountering a failure during migration with an OpenVZ container. The following is the error output that you might get during the migration:

```
suspend...
Cannot suspend container: Resource temporarily unavailable
Error: foreign process 554/523862(vzctl) inside CT (e.g. vzctl enter or
vzctl exec).
Error: suspend is impossible now.
```

Root cause: During the system migration for an OpenVZ container, the VM will be suspended. The output of a failed suspension is shown in the preceding code. It tells us that the resource is temporarily unavailable because Proxmox tries to reallocate the container to the target server, but it cannot be done because there is a user that is accessing the container with the vzctl enter command. Visit http://goo.gl/P3P1iv for more information.

Solution: To solve this problem, log out the user that is using vzctl to enter a command. You can check whether there is such a process by issuing the following command at the Proxmox node:

```
vzctl exec <VMID> | ps aux | grep vzctl
```

Prevention: Ensure that you do not enter the container if you want to perform system migration.

Now, I will show you the storage problems I have faced.

Troubleshooting system storage problems

In the previous chapters, we introduced three different storage systems, namely GlusterFS, CEPH, and DRBD volumes. In this section, I will list out the problems I have encountered while building the system for each separate filesystem.

DRBD volume not in synchronization

During a normal operation, data synchronization should be automatically performed. However, there are different scenarios that will cause a synchronization problem. The following problems will be covered in this section:

- Need access to up-to-date data

- Node with Diskless status
- Node with Unknown status

Need access to up-to-date data during service initialization

Root cause: Your system might indicate that the data inside the current node (in the following example, `vmsrv02`) is not up to date, and the resynchronization does not take place probably because of the timeout.

Solution: So, we need to tell the DRBD service to copy data from a peer node by overwriting the data in the current node. Assume that we have a DRBD resource, `r1`, defined as follows:

```
root@vmsrv02# drbdadm -- --discard-my-data connect r1
```

As of DRBD 8.4, we have a new syntax:

```
root@vmsrv02# drbdadm connect --discard-my-data r1
```

If this does not help, try to issue the following command on the healthy node `vmsrv01`:

```
root@vmsrv01# drbdadm -- --overwrite-data-of-peer primary r1
```

As of DRBD 8.4, we also have a new syntax for this command:

```
root@vmsrv01# drbdadm primary --force r1
```

Prevention: Normally, this problem occurs when there is a network delay between the DRBD nodes. Ensuring the connectivity between them will reduce the chance of getting this error.

DRBD volume shows the Diskless status

Symptom: You might encounter the following output when you check your DRBD service status:

```
m:res  cs          ro                ds                 p
1:r1   Connected   Primary/Primary   Diskless/UpToDate  C
```

Root cause: Normally, this error indicates that there is a disk I/O problem on the local DRBD node. Refer to this article for more information: `http://goo.gl/vwPcYN`. If you confirm that your hard drives are healthy, perform the operation provided in the solution.

Solution: Since both nodes are connected and one node shows the **UpToDate** status, we can easily fix this by restarting the DRBD service for the peer node showing the **Diskless** status using the following code:

```
root@vmsrv02# /etc/init.d/drbd restart

Stopping all DRBR resources:.
Starting DRBD resources: [ d(r1) s(r1) n(r1) ].
```

The peer node will become the primary node again if we check the service status, and the data will be synchronized from the healthy DRBD node:

```
root@vmsrv01# /etc/init.d/drbd status

m:res   cs                    ro                ds                          p
...     sync'ed:              0.9%              (10148/10236)               M
1:r1    SyncTarget            Primary/Primary   Inconsistent/UpToDate       C
```

When synchronization is complete, the DRBD volume operates normally.

Prevention: This error shows that there is an I/O problem on the local node, so make sure your local hard drive is operating normally. As DRBD highly depends on network connectivity, the network availability is also important.

DRBD volume shows the Unknown status

Symptom: You will receive the following output when you check the DRBD status in this situation:

```
m:res   cs                    ro                ds                     p
1:r1    WFConnection          Primary/Unknown   UpToDate/DUnknown      C
```

Root cause: It simply tells you that your node (for example, vmsrv01) is working properly with the up-to-date data, but the peer node (for example, vmsrv02) is either under a system failure or its network is disconnected. Therefore, the connection status for vmsrv01 changes to **WFConnection**, which indicates that it is waiting for the connection of the peer node, and data resynchronization is needed.

Solution: If the resynchronization doesn't take place when vmsrv02 is back online, you need to perform the following steps to solve the problem:

```
root@vmsrv02# drbdadm secondary r1
```

```
root@vmsrv02# drbdadm disconnect r1
```

```
root@vmsrv02# drbdadm --discard-my-data connect r1
```

For DRBD 8.4, we have the following new syntax:

```
root@vmsrv02# drbdadm connect --discard-my-data r1
```

If the result of the service status on vmsrv01 is similar to the following output, then vmsrv01 is running as the standalone mode:

```
m:res   cs            ro                ds                    p
1:r1    Standalone    Primary/Unknown   UpToDate/DUnknown     C
```

As vmsrv01 is not waiting for the peer node to connect and is running as a standalone mode, we have to issue the following command:

```
root@vmsrv01# drbdadm connect r1
```

The data should then be replicated from vmsrv01 to vmsrv02. If this does not happen, you can restart the DRBD service in vmsrv02 using the following command:

```
root@vmsrv02# /etc/init.d/drbd restart
```

Prevention: This error only appears if the network connectivity from the affected node (vmsrv02) is lost. So, make sure that the network is available to prevent this error.

Rebuilding a DRBD volume

In most circumstances, the automatic and manual recovery methods mentioned in the preceding section should solve the DRBD volume problem. If they don't, you could first back up the data in your volume and then rebuild the volume. To do this, follow these steps:

1. Back up the data in the DRBD volume to other locations, for example, /drbd-backup.

2. Stop the DRBD system service on both nodes using the following command:
   ```
   root@vmsrv01# /etc/init.d/drbd stop
   root@vmsrv02# /etc/init.d/drbd stop
   ```

3. Remove the partition used in the DRBD volume on *both* the nodes with the fdisk command, for example, /dev/sdd1:
   ```
   root@vmsrv01# fdisk /dev/sdd

   Command (m for help): d
   Partition number (1-4): 1
   Command (m for help): w
   ```

   Repeat the steps in vmsrv02.

4. Create a partition for the DRBD volume for use on both the nodes, as shown in the following command:

```
root@vmsrv01# fdisk /dev/sdd

Command (m for help): c
Partition number (1-4): 1
Command (m for help): w
```

Repeat the steps in vmsrv02.

5. Follow the instructions to create the DRBD volume mentioned in *Chapter 4, Configuring a Proxmox VE Cluster*.

In the next section, we will discuss the problems I came across with the Gluster filesystem during my system setup, which are listed as follows:

- Missing extended attribute trusted.glusterfs.volume-id
- Replacing a failed Gluster node

Failed to get the extended attribute trusted.glusterfs.volume-id for brick x on a GlusterFS volume

Root cause: Before we can go deep into this problem, we need to know whether the extended file and folder attributes are applied in the GlusterFS volume on top of the normal permission settings. Therefore, if these attributes are missing by accident or get replaced by a new hard drive, we will not be able to turn on this volume brick.

Solution: So, we need to perform the following steps to add the attributes back to the GlusterFS volume. Assume that we have a Gluster volume named glustertest and we set up a directory named /glusterfs-data/mount1 as the storage for the volume:

1. We need to stop the Gluster daemon service on all the nodes:

```
root@glusterFS1# service glusterd stop
```

2. In the affected node, we need to issue the following command to restore the extended file attribute, which is missing for the brick:

```
root@glusterFS1# (vol=glustertest; brick=/glusterfs-data/mount1; \
setfattr -n trusted.glusterfs.volume-id -v "$(grep volume-id \
/var/lib/glusterd/vols/$vol/info | cut -d= -f2 | \
sed 's/-//g')" $brick)
```

In this command, we have defined the Gluster volume name and the brick name with the variables `vol` and `brick`. Then, we make use of these two variables with `grep volume-id` from the Gluster info (`/var/lib/glusterd/vols/glustertest/info`) file, and remove the hyphens from the value. After that, we assign the new file attribute `trusted.glusterfs.volume-id` with this new `volume-id` to the brick (`/glusterfs-data/mount1`).

The Gluster info file contains the volume identifier (`volume-id`), number of replicas, the brick information, and so on. A sample info file is given as follows for your reference:

```
type=2
count=3
status=1
sub_count=3
stripe_count=1
replica_count=3
version=2
transport-type=0
volume-id=3f5f5433-7436-4592-8925-a686ca972281
username=3948ce10-81b5-4298-9371-fa317dfc11bb
password=c1740e99-3c16-4949-afe5-b9b5408df443
op-version=2
client-op-version=2
brick-0=192.168.1.51:-glusterfs-data-mount1
brick-1=192.168.1.52:-glusterfs-data-mount1
brick-2=192.168.1.53:-glusterfs-data-mount1
```

3. Then, we can start the Gluster daemon service in *all* the nodes:

```
root@glusterFS1# /etc/init.d/glusterd start
```

Note that this method should also solve the *GlusterFS volume ID mismatch for bricks* problem that we encountered during system start. Refer to this website as a solution for this problem: `http://goo.gl/dvCiYK`.

Prevention: Normally, this problem will only occur when you have accidentally removed the brick directory but created it again without applying the extended file attribute to it. Avoid removing the bricks simply with the `rm` command; or, use the following command:

```
gluster volume remove-brick glustertest 192.168.1.57:/glusterfs-data/
mount1
```

Replacing a failed Gluster node

Assume that we have a three-node Gluster system that contains glusterFS1, glusterFS2, and glusterFS3; glusterFS3 fails and is replaced with a new one. The steps to finish the replacement process are as follows:

1. On either glusterFS1 or glusterFS2, we need to find the UUID of the original glusterFS3:

   ```
   root@glusterFS1# grep glusterFS3 /var/lib/glusterd/peers/*
   ```

   You should receive a result similar to the one shown as follows:

   ```
   /var/lib/glusterd/peers/700558a5-fb4b-444c-869d-638bf37bfb84:hostn
   ame1=glusterFS3
   ```

2. After you have installed the GlusterFS packages on the glusterFS3 server, make sure that you have stopped the glusterd service using the following command:

   ```
   root@glusterFS3# /etc/init.d/glusterd stop
   ```

3. Then, we need to restore the UUID value 700558a5-fb4b-444c-869d-638bf37bfb84 back to the Gluster information file in glusterFS3:

   ```
   echo UUID={700558a5-fb4b-444c-869d-638bf37bfb84} > \
   /var/lib/glusterd/glusterd.info
   ```

4. Restore the extended file attribute to the shared brick on glusterFS3:

   ```
   root@glusterFS3# (vol=glustertest; brick=/glusterfs-data/mount1; \
   setfattr -n trusted.glusterfs.volume-id -v "$(grep volume-id \
   /var/lib/glusterd/vols/$vol/info | cut -d= -f2 | \
   sed 's/-//g')" $brick)
   ```

   This command is the same as the one listed before. It actually restores the extended file attribute by getting back the volume-info information from the *Gluster info* file, /var/lib/glusterd/vols/glustertest/info, and assigns the value back to the brick directory. For more details, read the *Failed to get extended attribute trusted.glusterfs.volume-id for brick x on a GlusterFS volume* section.

5. Start the glusterd service on glusterFS3 to make it back to the Gluster system:

   ```
   root@glusterFS3# /etc/init.d/glusterd start
   ```

In the next section, we are going to run through the following CEPH service errors as shown:

- Pipe fault during the CEPH service start up
- Degraded CEPH storage that shows OSD.x is down

CEPH service that shows AA.BB.CC.DD/0 pipe (XXX).fault

Symptom: When the CEPH service is starting, it will check whether all the CEPH monitors are started up or not. If there is one failure on the monitor node, the following symptom will be outputted on the system terminal:

```
2014-04-24 16:43:26.139718 7f6eb0293700   0 -- :/1180718 >>
192.168.1.58:6789/0 pipe(0x2847860 sd=4 :0 s=1 pgs=0 cs=0 l=1
c=0x2847ac0).fault
```

Root cause and solution: In this example, we found that the monitor service at `192.168.1.58` is not running, so we only need to start the monitor service at `vmsrv02` (assuming that the monitor service is named `mon.1`):

```
root@vmsrv02# pveceph start mon.1
```

Prevention: Make sure that the CEPH monitor service is running and operating normally.

CEPH service that shows OSD.X is down

Symptom: When we check the CEPH service status, you might find that the CEPH storage is in a degraded status, as shown in the following screenshot:

health	HEALTH_WARN 298 pgs degraded;
quorum	Yes {0 1 2}
cluster	1f31d573-0e14-47d2-b519-23e2c4ac542b
monmap	e5: 3 mons at 0=192.168.1.57:6789/0,1=192.168.1.58:6789/0,2=192.168.1.59:6789/0,
osdmap	e1292: 7 osds: 3 up, 3 in

Root cause: If you take a further look at the preceding screenshot, you will notice that there are some problems with the OSDs because there are only three out of seven OSDs active.

Solution: We have to solve the failure on the OSDs to get the CEPH service to run properly:

1. We need to check the **OSD** page for more details; you might find that there is an OSD listed in the CEPH storage but with the **down** state, as shown in the following screenshot:

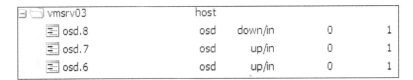

vmsrv03	host			
osd.8	osd	down/in	0	1
osd.7	osd	up/in	0	1
osd.6	osd	up/in	0	1

2. In this situation, you need to check the status of the corresponding physical hard drive under the **Disks** page, shown as follows:

/dev/sdc	osd.6	10.00GB	FreeBSD
/dev/sdd	osd.7	10.00GB	FreeBSD
/dev/sde	osd.8	10.00GB	FreeBSD

3. Next, you need to check whether we have a physical disk in /dev/sde and fix the problem. Once you have solved the physical disk problem, you can simply click on the **Start** button at the top menu to add your storage back to CEPH.

    If your hard drive cannot be recovered, you can consider removing this entry from the CEPH storage.

4. First, you need to choose the target OSD drive (for example, **osd.8**) and click on the **Out** button in the top menu:

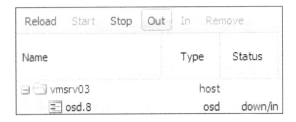

Reload	Start	Stop	Out	In	Remove
Name				Type	Status
vmsrv03				host	
osd.8				osd	down/in

5. When the status of **osd.8** is changed to **down/out**, you can click on the **Remove** button in the top menu.

6. Click on **Remove** to clear the **osd.8** entry from CEPH, as shown in the following screenshot:

You have successfully removed the damaged hard drive from the CEPH storage, and of course, you can add another hard drive with the name **osd.8** afterwards.

Prevention: This error is normally caused due to disk failure in the CEPH storage; make sure that you have a healthy hard drive to prevent this error.

Now, I will share with you some troubleshooting experiences with cluster service failure.

Troubleshooting Proxmox cluster problems

In this section, we will go through some common problems that we encounter during the operation of a Proxmox cluster, which are as follows:

- HA VM start up problem
- The fenced cluster node cannot recover automatically
- The cluster member node cannot join back with the cluster
- The cluster service cannot be restarted because of the DLM lockspace
- Activity blocked within the cluster

Unable to start the HA-enabled VM

Symptom: When you try to start an HA-enabled VM, the operation fails with the following output:

```
Executing HA start for VM 201
Member vmsrv01 trying to enable pvevm:201... Aborted; service failed
TASK ERROR: command 'clusvcadm -e pvevm:201 -m vmsrv01' failed: exit code
254
```

Root cause: So, if you start the HA-enabled VM again, the process will still be unsuccessful with the same output. The problem is that the VM 201 is in the **failed** status, and so it cannot be turned on:

HA Service Status		
Name	Owner	Status
pvevm:201	none	failed

Solution: The HA service with the failed status cannot be used until we re-enable it, so we need to perform the following steps:

1. To solve the problem, we need to disable this **HA service** first with the following:

    ```
    root@vmsrv01# clusvadm -d pvevm:201

    Local machine disabling pvevm:201...Success
    ```

2. After that, you can verify that the status of this service is changed to **disabled**:

HA Service Status		
Name	Owner	Status
pvevm:201	none	disabled

3. You should be able to turn on the VM either from the web management console or with the command line:

    ```
    root@vmsrv01# clusvadm -e pvevm:201
    ```

Prevention: An HA service will be marked as failed because it cannot be run on both the cluster nodes. Make sure that you have enough system resources for the HA service in terms of CPU, memory, and most importantly, the status of the shared storage resource.

The cluster node is being fenced

Symptom: The first thing you will notice is that the cluster node is shown in the *red icon* and is *offline* in the **Summary** page in the web management console. In this example, the fenced node is vmsrv02:

Another symptom is that many error messages will appear in the failed node when you check using the dmesg command:

```
sd 8:0:0:0: rejecting I/O to offline device
```

If you have configured your quorum disk, you can still create a new VM. However, when you further check the cluster status in the command-line interface with the pvecm command, you will find that the node is not in a cluster:

```
root@vmsrv01# pvecm nodes

Node  Sts  Inc   Joined                  Name
   0  M      0   2014-07-05 04:21:38     /dev/block/8:16
   1  M   5820   2014-07-05 04:20:48     vmsrv01
   2  X   5824                           vmsrv02
```

The X sign under the Sts column means that vmsrv02 is not available. Since we have configured a quorum disk, the cluster is still operational, as shown in the following command and its output:

```
root@vmsrv01# pvecm status

Cluster Name: mycluster
Cluster Member: Yes
Membership state: Cluster-Member
Nodes: 1
Expected votes: 3
Quorum device votes: 1
Total votes: 2
Node votes: 1
Quorum: 2
Node name: vmsrv01
Node ID: 1
```

Root cause: Due to network connectivity problems or system failure, the cluster node is being fenced from the cluster.

Solution: To solve this problem, we need to issue the following command on `vmsrv01`:

```
root@vmsrv01# fence_node vmsrv02 -U
```

Then, the server `vmsrv02` will be restarted; the normal cluster operation is resumed when the cluster node comes back online, as shown in the following screenshot:

Datacenter	Search	Summary	Options	Storage	Backup	Users	Groups

Nodes

Name	ID	Online	Support	Estranged	Server Address	Services
vmsrv01	1	Yes	-	No	192.168.47.1	PVECluster
vmsrv02	2	Yes	-	No	192.168.47.2	PVECluster

Prevention: Ensure that your Proxmox node is equipped with multiple network cards to provide network redundancy; having redundancy in power supplies will greatly reduce the chance of getting into this problem.

Nodes unable to rejoin cluster after fence or reboot

Root cause: After a system reboot or after recovering from a network failure, a cluster node might not be able to join back with the cluster domain. One of the possible reasons for this is the inconsistency of the cluster configuration file. During a normal operation, cluster configuration content is synchronized via the *corosync* service that ensures data consistency.

When we make changes to the cluster configuration file in `vmsrv01`, corosync will also update the file at `vmsrv02`, as shown in the following command and its output:

```
root@vmsrv01:/etc/pve# ls -la
-rw-r----- 1 root www-data 2220 Jul  7 20:57 cluster.conf
root@vmsrv02:/etc/pve# ls -la
-rw-r----- 1 root www-data 2220 Jul  7 20:57 cluster.conf
```

When there is a high network latency or network failure, then the synchronization process might fail if both the cluster nodes attempt to change the content of the cluster configuration file at `/etc/pve/cluster.conf`.

If the configuration file is out of synchronization, the cluster node without the latest update will not be able to start the cluster service, as shown in the following output:

```
Starting cluster:
   Checking if cluster has been disabled at boot... [  OK  ]
   Checking Network Manager... [  OK  ]
   Global setup... [  OK  ]
   Loading kernel modules... [  OK  ]
   Mounting configfs... [  OK  ]
   Starting cman... [  OK  ]
   Waiting for quorum... Timed-out waiting for cluster
```

Solution: To solve this problem, we need to make the affected node (vmsrv02) acquire the updated content of the cluster configuration file by copying the content from another node (vmsrv01). Then, we should be able to join vmsrv02 back with the cluster using the following command:

```
root@vmsrv02# /etc/init.d/cman restart

Starting cluster:
Checking if cluster has been disabled at boot... [  OK  ]
   Checking Network Manager... [  OK  ]
   Global setup... [  OK  ]
   Loading kernel modules... [  OK  ]
   Mounting configfs... [  OK  ]
   Starting cman... [  OK  ]
   Starting qdiskd... [  OK  ]
   Waiting for quorum... [  OK  ]
   Starting fenced... [  OK  ]
   Starting dlm_controld... [  OK  ]
   Tuning DLM kernel config... [  OK  ]
   Unfencing self... [  OK  ]
   Joining fence domain... [  OK  ]
```

Prevention: There are two possible reasons that cause the cluster.conf file to be out of sync with the cluster member nodes, and they are as follows:

- First, you manually edit the content of the cluster.conf file that will have a great chance of harming your cluster, leading to a cluster failure. The correct method to update the configuration is to create a new cluster.conf.new file from the original cluster.conf file and activate the changes under the GUI console.

- Another possible reason also mentioned before is to make sure that you have a reliable network that can help you avoid this kind of error.

Unable to restart the cluster service

Symptom: In some situations, you may want to restart the local cluster service with the following command:

```
root@vmsrv01# /etc/init.d/cman restart
```

However, the operation fails and you receive an output similar to the following output:

```
Stopping cluster:
Leaving fence domain... found dlm lockspace /sys/kernel/dlm/rgmanager
fence_tool: cannot leave due to active systems
[FAILED]
```

Root cause: The reason for this error is that there is a DLM lockspace for rgmanager. We can perform a further check with the dlm_tool or cman_tool commands, shown as follows:

```
root@vmsrv01# dlm_tool ls
```

We can also use the following:

```
root@vmsrv01# cman_tool services
```

Now, we will get the following output:

```
dlm lockspaces
name          rgmanager
id            0x5231f3eb
flags         0x00000000
change        member 2 joined 1 remove 0 failed 0 seq 2,2
members       1 2
```

Solution: As we found from the preceding result, there is a locking status in the rgmanager process. We need to perform the following action to solve this problem:

1. As rgmanager requires a lock operation between the cluster members, we need to stop it from escaping from the locking scheme using the following command:

   ```
   root@vmsrv01# /etc/init.d/rgmanager stop
   ```

2. Then, we should be able to restart the cluster manager (cman) on the target member node:

   ```
   root@vmsrv01# /etc/init.d/cman restart
   ```

3. Next, we can start the `rgmanager` service:

```
root@vmsrv01# /etc/init.d/rgmanager start
```

4. Finally, you might need to restart the Proxmox filesystem service (`pve-cluster`):

```
root@vmsrv01# /etc/init.d/pve-cluster restart
```

Unable to perform any change on the cluster

As there are not enough node members in the cluster, any activity changed on the cluster will be blocked, as shown in the following command and its output:

```
root@srv01# pvecm status

Cluster Name: mycluster
Cluster Member: Yes
Membership state: Cluster-Member
Nodes: 2
Expected votes: 3
Total votes: 2
Node votes: 1
Quorum: 2 Activity blocked
```

In such a circumstance, we need to make sure that the available cluster member nodes are at least equal to the number of *Expected votes*.

Summary

In this chapter, we listed out some common problems and solutions that we might face during daily operation, from system access problems to the actual cluster-related problems for a Proxmox cluster. Of course, I cannot list out all the circumstances that would cause the problem, but we can list some ideas by checking the system log files under the following paths:

- `/var/log/messages`
- `/var/log/syslog`
- `/var/log/cluster/qdiskd.log`
- `/var/log/cluster/corosync.log`
- `/var/log/cluster/dlm_controld.log`
- `/var/log/cluster/fenced.log`
- `/var/log/cluster/rgmanager.log`

If you have read through this book, I have no doubt that you have learned not only the practical techniques, but also the background concepts behind this software. Proxmox is an open source virtualization tool that comes with amazing functionalities. If you are new to virtualization, Proxmox would be a good starting point for you to catch a glimpse of how system administrators or developers work when creating a cluster system.

Index

URL 111, 113
used, for handling server failure 53
graphical user interface (GUI) 14, 115
guest OS 10

H

HA
achieving, strategies 32
HA environment
about 29
availability 30
HA-protected VM
building 130-133
hardware-assisted virtualization (HV) 9
HA service relocation
KVM relocation, testing 135
OpenVZ container relocation,
testing on 134, 135
testing on 134
heartbeat, HA
about 33
first condition 33
second condition 33
High Availability. *See* **HA**
host OS 10
HyperTerminal 102
hypervisor
about 5
comparing, virtualization platforms
based 12
Hyper-V server
comparing, with server virtualization
software 11

I

IBM
URL 63
Intelligent Platform Management
Interface (IPMI) 64
iSCSI-based storage option
advantages 57
disadvantages 58
iSCSI device
about 83
device extent 83
file extent 83

iSCSI initiator 83
iSCSI portal 83
iSCSI target 83
LUN (logical unit number) 83
working with 84-86
iSCSI initiator 83
iSCSI portal 83
iSCSI shared storage
device 83-86
preparing, with NAS4free 82
ISO file
uploading, to Proxmox 14, 15
ISO image option 15

K

Kernel-based Virtual Machine. *See* **KVM**
key components, for building Proxmox VE
Cluster
fencing device 61
quorum disk 66
reliable network 60
shared storage 47
Kpartx, command-line tool 153
KVM
about 23
backing up, with vzdump stop
mode 175, 176
creating 18-21
restoring, with vzrestore 188-190
using, with live migration 128, 129

L

Linux platform
system migration 144
live migration
about 36, 124
KVM, using 128, 129
OpenVZ container, using 125-127
post-copy memory migration 36
pre-copy memory migration 36-38
live migration preparation, of physical
machine
data, copying from source server to
Proxmox server 155-157
on Proxmox server 152, 153
on source machine 149, 150

live migration preparation, on Proxmox server
  about 152
  disk information, restoring on source backup 153-155
live migration preparation, on source machine
  about 149
  LVM snapshot volume, creating for data copying 150, 151
load balancing, HA 32
Logical Volume Manager. *See* LVM
LUN (logical unit number) 83
lvcreate command 151
LVM
  about 50, 51
  creating 50
  volumes, adding 51
LVM logical volume
  size, reducing 180, 181
LVM shared storage
  storage preparation 123
LVM snapshot
  used, for backing up 182
  using, with vzdump 178
LVM volume
  based on DRBD shared storage, creating 98
  for backup storage, creating 179
  physical storage, adding 181, 182
  physical storage, replacing 181, 182

M

Master Boot Record (MBR) 150
MDS map 57
minicom
  about 102
  URL 102
monitor map 56

N

NAS4free
  used, for iSCSI shared storage preparation 82
negative effects, system downtime
  customer trust loss 31
  internal staff productivity reduction 32

system recovery 31
network
  building, with redundancy 69
  configuring, for Proxmox VE cluster 69
  preparing, for Proxmox cluster 80-82
network address translation (NAT) 71
Network-attached storage (NAS) 48
network fencing
  about 63
  using, with Cisco switch via SNMP 101-108
network options, Proxmox
  bonding interface 70
  bridged interface 70
  NAT interface 70
  routed interface 70
network, Proxmox VE cluster
  bonding device 76
  building, with redundancy 70
  configuring 69
  DRBD 77
  infrastructure, creating 74
  quorum device 75
  separate network, building 70
  VLAN structure 71
NIC teaming 76

O

object, Ceph storage 55
object storage devices (OSD) 117
OpenVZ (Open Virtuozzo)
  about 10, 23, 24
  supported operating system 24
OpenVZ-based virtual machine
  creating 16, 17
OpenVZ container
  backing up, with vzdump stop mode 172
  restoring, with vzrestore 185-188
  using, for live migration 125-127
OpenVZ template
  about 15, 25
  building, from existing container 195-197
  downloading 25, 26
  URL, for downloading 25, 145
operation types, clone mode
  full clone 198
  linked clone 198

Thank you for buying
Proxmox High Availability

About Packt Publishing

Packt, pronounced 'packed', published its first book "*Mastering phpMyAdmin for Effective MySQL Management*" in April 2004 and subsequently continued to specialize in publishing highly focused books on specific technologies and solutions.

Our books and publications share the experiences of your fellow IT professionals in adapting and customizing today's systems, applications, and frameworks. Our solution based books give you the knowledge and power to customize the software and technologies you're using to get the job done. Packt books are more specific and less general than the IT books you have seen in the past. Our unique business model allows us to bring you more focused information, giving you more of what you need to know, and less of what you don't.

Packt is a modern, yet unique publishing company, which focuses on producing quality, cutting-edge books for communities of developers, administrators, and newbies alike. For more information, please visit our website: www.packtpub.com.

About Packt Open Source

In 2010, Packt launched two new brands, Packt Open Source and Packt Enterprise, in order to continue its focus on specialization. This book is part of the Packt Open Source brand, home to books published on software built around Open Source licenses, and offering information to anybody from advanced developers to budding web designers. The Open Source brand also runs Packt's Open Source Royalty Scheme, by which Packt gives a royalty to each Open Source project about whose software a book is sold.

Writing for Packt

We welcome all inquiries from people who are interested in authoring. Book proposals should be sent to author@packtpub.com. If your book idea is still at an early stage and you would like to discuss it first before writing a formal book proposal, contact us; one of our commissioning editors will get in touch with you.

We're not just looking for published authors; if you have strong technical skills but no writing experience, our experienced editors can help you develop a writing career, or simply get some additional reward for your expertise.

open source *
community experience distilled

Getting Started with Oracle VM VirtualBox

Getting Started with Oracle
VM VirtualBox

Build your own virtual environment from scratch using VirtualBox

Pradyumna Dash

[PACKT] enterprise

Getting Started with Oracle VM VirtualBox

ISBN: 978-1-78217-782-1   Paperback: 86 pages

Build your own virtual environment from scratch using VirtualBox

1. Learn how to install, configure, and manage VirtualBox.

2. A step-by-step guide which will teach you how to build your own virtual environment from scratch.

3. Discover advanced features of VirtualBox.

Getting Started with
XenDesktop® 7.x

Craig Thomas Ellrod

[PACKT] enterprise

Getting Started with XenDesktop® 7.x

ISBN: 978-1-84968-976-2   Paperback: 422 pages

Deliver desktops and applications to your end users, anywhere, anytime, with XenDesktop® 7.x

1. Build a complete and secure XenDesktop 7 site from the ground up.

2. Discover how to virtualize and deliver accessible desktops and applications to your end users.

3. Full of clear, step-by-step instructions with screenshots, which will walk you through the entire process of XenDesktop site creation.

Please check **www.PacktPub.com** for information on our titles

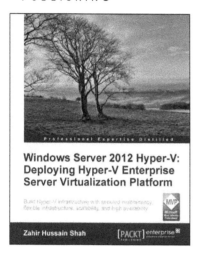

Windows Server 2012 Hyper-V: Deploying Hyper-V Enterprise Server Virtualization Platform

ISBN: 978-1-84968-834-5   Paperback: 410 pages

Build Hyper-V infrastructure with secured multitenancy, flexible infrastructure, scalability, and high availability

1. A complete step-by-step Hyper-V deployment guide, covering all Hyper-V features for configuration and management best practices.

2. Understand multi-tenancy, flexible architecture, scalability, and high availability features of new Windows Server 2012 Hyper-V.

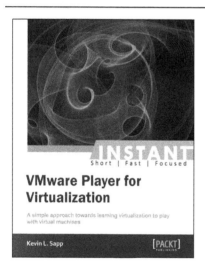

Instant VMware Player for Virtualization

ISBN: 978-1-84968-984-7   Paperback: 84 pages

A simple approach towards learning virtualization to play with virtual machines

1. Learn something new in an Instant! A short, fast, focused guide delivering immediate results.

2. Discover the latest features of VMware Player 5.0.

3. Evaluate new technology without paying for additional hardware costs.

4. Test your applications in an isolated environment.

www.ingramcontent.com/pod-product-compliance
Lightning Source LLC
Chambersburg PA
CBHW060538060326

40690CB00017B/3532